ENGLAND
BY
BICYCLE

Bicycling: A History
The Comic Postcard in English Life
The Inland Resorts and Spas of Britain
The New Grand Tour: Travelling Today through
Europe, Asia Minor, India and Nepal
View North: A Long Look at Northern England

ENGLAND
BY
BICYCLE

FREDERICK   ALDERSON

Distributed by
SELPRESS BOOKS
16 BERKELEY STREET
D /   LONDON, W1X 6AP
NEWTON ABBOT   LONDON
NORTH POMFRET (VT) VANCOUVER

0 7153 6432 4

Set in 11 on 13 Linotype Baskerville and printed in
Great Britain by Devonshire Press Limited, Torquay, Devon
for David & Charles (Holdings) Limited
South Devon House Newton Abbot Devon

Published in the United States of America
by David & Charles Inc North Pomfret
Vermont   05053   USA

Published in Canada by Douglas David &
Charles Limited 3645 McKechnie Drive
West Vancouver BC

CONTENTS

LIST OF ILLUSTRATIONS

Unless otherwise acknowledged the photographs are reproduced by courtesy of Barnaby's Picture Library

Quotations used at the head of each chapter are taken from 'Golden Hints for Cyclists', *The Rambler* (1897)

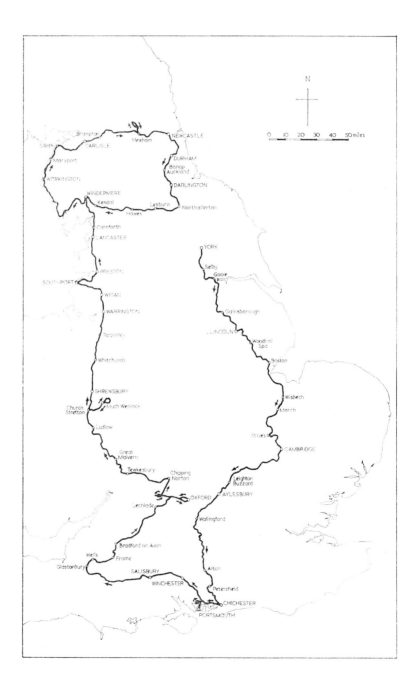

INTRODUCTION

JUST off the roaring, high-velocity motorways and the congested main roads, there is still a leisurely, low-decibel, cyclists' England. Here, quite apart from national parks, conservation areas and other tourists' high spots, is an unspectacular, intimate countryside: and it is the cyclist, himself unspectacular, not the motorist, who is best equipped to enjoy its pleasures of pub, church, market-place and cottage in all their variety of regional character. Here, on occasion he can still enjoy being 'king of the road', seventy years after the heyday of the bicycle—and enjoy it all the more for that.

When I set off, a year or so ago, to look round England on a bicycle I was not so confident in this belief. Friends and acquaintances, motorists to a man, were certain that the noise, fumes and speed of modern traffic would drive me off the road before I was half-way round—unscathed perhaps, if I was exceptionally lucky. They thought it a foolhardy undertaking, a potential menace to other road users' (ie, their own) safety and, in any case, not worth the effort.

Since cycling had not been my exercise for a score of years and in case there was some ground for these friendly warnings, I chose to make a start on the quieter side of England. There would, I thought, be less heavy traffic in the agricultural eastern counties, less distraction, less leg strain.

There are no hills, of course, that you'd call hills
And yet the land's not flat: it swells
In folds of green, climbs slopes of brown
Unfurls long yellow swathes of corn
From dust-white roads up to the waiting sky.

There are no hills, but sometimes knolls of trees
Stand high and cast from field to field
Their evening shade: sometimes a mill
Towers like a lighthouse and makes small
As any mountain prospect all the plain.

There was also here, I thought, the chance in early spring of a helpful wind whilst I tacked southerly and as I did so the weather should warm up.

In the USA experts now forecast the polarisation of population into three immense megalopolitan areas, continuous built-up regions of about 60,000,000 inhabitants—one from Boston to Washington, another round Chicago, the third from San Francisco to San Diego—whilst the rest of the country will be left practically empty, its smaller towns deserted, its cultivated areas run by huge combines. England, luckily, is not yet subject to population drifts of this order, but even so I decided to avoid the minor megalopolitan monsters, the Birmingham–Coventry area and the outliers of London, if only because of the monotony of the continuous built-up areas. As George Orwell wrote in *The Road to Wigan Pier,* 'as you travel northward your eye, accustomed to the South and East, does not notice much difference until you are beyond Birmingham. In Coventry you might as well be in Finsbury Park . . . and between all the towns of the Midlands there stretches a villa-civilisation indistinguishable from that of the South'.

Although few cyclists seek out urban routes for pleasure to see England representatively, some urban routes must not be shunned. I proposed to sample them as interludes from rusticity—in port, cathedral city, university and industrial town, seaside resort—somewhat in the spirit of Arnold Bennett escaping into Manchester 'as a prisoner escapes into the open country'.

'Small is beautiful, or the study of economics as if people mattered' is the text of many of us today in reaction to conurbation and industrial complexes, and 'slow is meaningful' could well be applied to modern personal transport. In human terms the journey matters as much as, if not more than, the destination. If you tour the Highlands of Scotland by bicycle you will come to know their beauties in a way you can never do by car—as any honest motorist who has done it both ways must admit. The faster you go the less you can take in and the less meaning attaches to the journey. The cyclist can stop and look as the motorist never does.

The bicycle, then, is unrivalled for touring; it is at its best on roads not planned as the shortest routes from one indistinguishable conurbation to another, but on those that wind and wander round field boundaries and old estates or that follow the curves of river or lake and link village to village. Such routes revert sometimes to 'green roads'—known only to countrymen and used by drover and gipsy. The cyclist here can stop on an impulse to admire a view, examine a flower or note a building—though, of course, he can 'move' when he wants to, keeping up his own or his group's rhythm.

The route I followed allowed me to indulge to the full in this kind of travel. I chose minor roads as much as possible, lingered in the less known rather than the tourist town, letting the chance of surprise rather than the certainly of a 'show-piece' high-light my day. And as it turned out, there were many parts of England, particularly in the West Midlands, the East and North, where unhurried travel led to far greater pleasures than the guidebooks suggest. Celebrated places these days can be a shade commonplace—rubbed smooth of their individuality by excess of custom.

I had to go through some parts, of course, where the pleasure of unhurried travel was ruled out: my impulse was to pedal on and get through. These were not necessarily the heavily industrialised regions where you know what to expect, but routes where the weight and tempo of traffic gave the cyclist the feeling that he was regarded as 'fair game', an unnecessary hazard to the more powerful, aggressive road-users. These parts, as often as not, had stretches that were too narrow or too wide by turns, or just badly maintained, affording minimum safety for the man on two wheels. On one or two occasions, I walked to avoid being 'winged'.

Nothing that has just been said, however, tips the balance against enjoyment of a cycling tour through England today. Immediacy of contact with all the country sights and sounds, with the oddities and endless beauties of by-road village, the placidity or weekly bustle of unsophisticated market town— this more than makes up for the occasional 'black spot' road or spoiled environment.

Attention is so often focused on encroachment, redevelopment, exploitation in particular areas—'a bit of Britain the size of the Isle of Wight disappears under concrete every year' (*Radio Times,* June 1973)—that the range and diversity of unchanged, uncommercialised, uncontaminated places in England with character or charm is often overlooked. A bicycle more than anything else helps one both to find and to appreciate them: they and it have quiet tastes in common.

And a bicycle leaves no smell, oil-drip, weakened fabric or frightened pedestrian in its wake. For this, if for no other reason, it seemed to me there was extra warmth in the welcome for the cyclist at almost every overnight halt on my journey.

> *Come then, you who couldn't stick it,*
> *lovers of cricket, underpaid journalists,*
> *lovers of Nature, hikers, O touring cyclists . . .*

as Rex Warner wrote in his '*Hymn*' (1933),

> *this is the beginning of good.*

CHAPTER ONE

EASTERN SKIES

A cycling tour marked by a modest average of miles per day is more beneficial to health than one associated with record speed and consequent nerve exhaustion.

I CHOSE to set off, practically a non-cyclist since the war, on a new 'semi-racer' machine acquired only a fortnight before, to make a month's continuous, fairly complete tour of England, from York on 1 April.

On the way to York by car, with my 'Claud Butler' lashed to the roof, its front wheel and saddle bags on the back seat, my driver and I became lost. Traffic circulation systems had changed, buildings altered or disappeared, new roundabouts mushroomed into being since last we had been there. At one complex roundabout, conscious of malfeasance, we pulled into the kerb while I sought guidance from a busy warden. His directions were clear, up to a point, but ended 'then ask again'.

When I had breasted the tide of traffic back to the kerb I became aware that a police patrol car was pulled in just ahead of ours. Before its occupant could swoop I hastened to explain.

'Oh, I know all about that,' the young constable broke in. 'You want Stockton Lane. Will you get in now and follow me.'

He eased smoothly out into the traffic, glanced to see whether we were with him, selected his lane, got to the lights just on green, took us neatly through several crossings, forked right and at the beginning of a long suburban avenue waved us down as he slowed to a halt.

'What number was it you wanted, Sir? This is the road.' I thought it better not to arrive at a friend's house conveyed by a police car and thanked him then and there, somewhat effusively.

'Oh, just part of the service,' said the young constable with a grin, glancing at my bicycle and then again at me. It seemed on reflection a good augury—and a good date—for taking to the road again after twenty-five years.

After a night's hospitality among friends and an apprehensive glance, early on, at the outside world—it had rained without pause for the previous forty-eight hours—I assembled 'Claud' and my baggage and was ready for off. It was a quiet, early-for-Sunday, Easter morning. Nobody was about. In order to see me, not lost, from the northern to the southern outskirts of York, one of my friends offered to cycle out for a mile or so alongside. He unearthed a rusting roadster from the garage, got in line ahead and, with waves all round to his family we pedalled off.

At least, he did. I had attempted to back-pedal the crank into a suitable position for a standing start and, unused to the Simplex—or indeed any other derailleur five-speed gear—in doing so dislodged the chain. By the time I had found a bit of garden cane to ease it back—not wanting oily hands quite so soon—and got properly into position, the roadster had disappeared from view. I was glad that nobody was about. Cutting out farewell waves this time, I caught up my creaking companion at the first crossing—but only by the luck of adverse traffic lights.

One of my reasons for choice of York as starting-point was that it is surrounded by so much flat country and gives access to country roads comparatively free of traffic. The idea was to find my legs and acclimatise to modern traffic stresses in easy conditions. So, heading south by east for Selby and Lincolnshire, I left York by its university suburb, the pleasant, one-street village-turned-campus, Fulford. From there the Naburn

Page 17 The author with his 'Claud Butler' at the start of his journey

Page 18 (left) The Shambles, York;
(above) en route

road, past Bishopthorpe and along the river Ouse as far as Cawood, was almost deserted. A mild air, a shy sun had followed the rain: the breeze blew from the south-west. I was apparently the only one abroad to enjoy this Easter morning —daffodils on the verges, golden willow and celandines in the ditches, skylarks trilling and bright mirrors of flood-water in the dark-chocolate plough. Tall hedges lined most of the road, an appreciable barrier against the wind which was driving clouds high up in the soft grey skies.

Bishopthorpe lies only three miles from York: otherwise I might have stopped for the Palace gardens, the avenue of seventeenth-century limes, the larches (some of the first introduced into England) and the manor-house Palace which has been the residence of archbishops of York for over seven hundred years. Instead I called a brief halt at Cawood. It was partly to see the former palace of archbishops, on the site of a castle built by the Saxon king Athelstan from which Bishopthorpe acquired its striking entrance gateway, partly, it must be admitted, to get out of the saddle.

The tall, white stone, fifteenth-century gatehouse, now linking a brick-built house to a barn, is all that remains of the palace here which Cardinal Wolsey intended should rival that of Hampton Court: the gateway was removed to Bishopthorpe in the mid-eighteenth century. The gatehouse comes as a complete surprise, just beyond the turn of the Selby road: Wolsey was arranging for three hundred men to work on improvements to the castle when he was removed from there under arrest by the Earl of Northumberland, to begin his final, fatal journey to Leicester. From it I walked back to look again at the broad cockling flood of the Ouse, which had been joined by the Wharfe only a mile or so upstream, and to admire, from the Toll Bridge, the curve of riverside cottages downstream. With its compact streets, tight little pubs, its moorings and meandering lanes, Cawood is a place for the fisherman to spin his own idyll on summer evenings.

I was loitering a bit for Cawood's sake—and for my own. When we were discussing 'Claud's' specifications the cycle

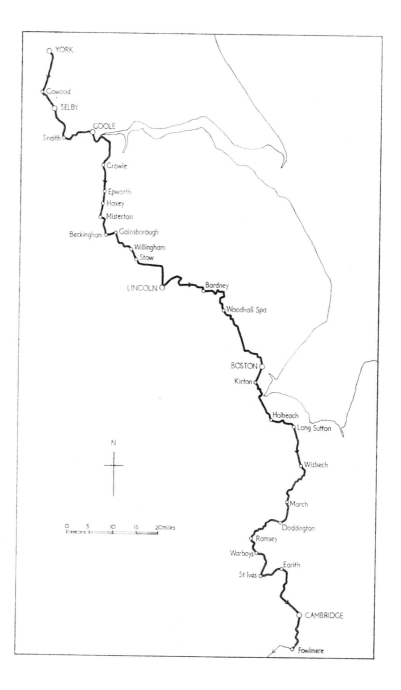

YORK
Cawood
SELBY
Snaith
GOOLE
Crowle
Epworth
Haxey
Misterton
Beckingham
Gainsborough
Willingham
Stow
LINCOLN
Bardney
Woodhall Spa
BOSTON
Kirton
Holbeach
Long Sutton
Wisbech
March
Doddington
Ramsey
Warboys
Earith
St Ives
CAMBRIDGE
Fowlmere

N

0   5   10   15   20miles

dealer had asked my choice of saddle. 'You either have leather,' he said, 'of the best quality that shapes itself to your seat with wear: or you have plastic. Plastic starts like iron, but it never warps, it's never wet and, in time, it will shape your seat to it. I know which I'd have if you really want to cycle.' So plastic it was—a slim Italian Unicanitor—and I suffered with it for the first few days. After that there was no more to it than in riding a trotting horse—one never seems to touch down long enough to ache.

The change in direction from Cawood towards Selby is roughly a right-angle and with it I now met the breeze head on. It was more wind, in fact, and there were no protective hedges on this stretch. I was glad of my gear ratio. After brief experiment I had had it extended in both directions—giving 92, 76, 71, 58, 49—and I settled into 58. I found it easier, at first, until I got the feel of the change lever, to go right down and then come up to find this particular gear. Apart from a couple of cyclists coming up fast the other way, traffic was negligible and the road to Selby somewhat featureless. Just as well in a way, since the road edges were rough and lumpy, a fault far too common to many both 'B' and 'A' roads, and one that militates against enjoying the view, whenever there is any density of traffic, as well as against riding comfort. But soon the towers of Selby Abbey and the silhouette of cooling towers—cathedrals of industry—rose into prominence.

Entry into Selby from this side is not impressive. Although surrounded by agricultural land, it seems to have been infected by the smoky atmosphere of towns a few miles to the west. The narrow street of old, soft-coloured red-brick houses looks grimy and impoverished. The long roof line and low central tower of the great abbey church, severely Norman and Early English in its western half, has not the elevation to break this monotonous impression. Inside, of course, the dark Norman aisles, sombre chancel, massive circular columns covered with grooved diaper-work and the ponderous arches of the abbey church founded by William the Conqueror have their own inalienable effect.

It was not a good time for sightseeing in Selby, which needs bustle to bring it to life. A rather blustery Sunday midday, the empty interregnum of the week that depersonalises most towns, and especially one that in spite of its industries, bricks, chemicals, flour-milling and rope making, remains essentially a market town. Among the few loungers in their lounge suits, waiting for opening time, I felt a shade conspicuous in my new Dalesman 'plusses', grey mixture stockings, long light blue sweater and Pakistani beret—this last knitted for me by a stallholder on the pattern of the close-fitting, ribbed white one worn by him to market. The two things that I lingered over may for this reason have been off-centre from the general interest. One was a common grave, near the abbey walk, in which a whole long list of mid-nineteenth-century victims of a cholera epidemic—'King Cholera' it was called before sanitation or slum clearance ousted it—were interred, all children under five. The other was the toll bridge which takes all traffic across the river to Hull or York, said to be the only one of its kind in England built of wood. Apart from this striking feature, the Ouse contributes little of charm to Selby, flowing sluggishly between its muddy banks and the various modern installations of a type anything but picturesque. The tower and lofty outworks of Rank's vast flour mill, just across the bridge, are impressive but grotesque.

So I pushed on, literally now, over the wide fertile plain— farmers' country growing some of our best corn—and nearly due south to Snaith and Goole. This is one of the least known, to outsiders, and least publicised parts of the West Riding, whose accepted character it challenges. In the Black Dog at Camblesforth, where the Drax road joins in, I could hardly have been further from the heavy woollens tradition. The company, with the ruddy glow of farming on their faces, 'cheese-cutter' caps on their heads and yellow ankle-boots, sat at dominoes or smoking placid pipes surrounded by a display of corn dollies, old guns, martingales, harness ornaments, riding boot-hooks and boot-stretchers enough to set up a folk museum. Their week's thirst was methodically quenched, the week's gossip quietly retailed as I followed my round of ham with another of cheese and onion. Here no one was made to feel a stranger in a strange land: country pub 'manners' means not looking.

It was a mistake, though, to have taken two rounds of sandwiches with my pint of bitter: one round is enough, with a half of shandy, for the cyclist who aims to use the afternoon refreshed, not replete. I let Snaith go by, grey church, red-roofed and red-brick houses, inns and shops not too self-aware of their antiquity—the township is mentioned three times in Domesday Book, had an ecclesiastical court of its own, and was once the eighth largest place in the West Riding—without fully registering its unusual quality. Snaith is part of a scene —highlighted again, a mile or two further on, by the charming double village green of Rawcliffe, fringed with chestnut trees and neat, freshly painted houses—that has the homely beauty of a Dutch painting. This is one of West Yorkshire's surprises, like Sedbergh, another out-of-the-way corner of the Riding, just seventy-five miles distant as the crow flies.

The wind was in my favour on the next bit to Goole. I could cruise along in carefree euphoria and exchange perhaps over-hearty greetings with the group of nine or ten 'wheelers', heads down and faces dark red, making heavy going of it in the other direction. Goole's leafy outskirts and grammar school, suburban shops and terraces looked cheerful in mild afternoon sun: on a market day I would have lingered to enjoy what sailors call 'Sleepy Hollow'. The real, in fact the only attraction, came when I turned right-angled again, at the road junction, and confronted the West Riding's only port. Big vessels from Bremen, Hamburg, Amsterdam, Copenhagen lay up just behind the houses. This was a fishing village until 1826, but the Don flows here into the tidal Ouse and after the Aire and Calder Navigation Company opened a canal linking it with the Aire, the heavy industries and pits of south Yorkshire used it as their outlet to the sea. Its subsequent importance for foreign trade can be measured by the size of the docks. This quietish unremarkable town is perhaps the one place in the Riding where the 'trespass of alien habits' and the odd accent of an incomer receive matter-of-course acceptance. You don't have to speak her language to take a girl to the cinema in Goole or keep a restaurant to keep face if you are Chinese.

The Don, as it comes into Old Goole, has been called Dutch river ever since Vermuyden deepened its channel and raised its banks in Charles I's day: the villages along the Ouse, Reedness, Whitgift, Ousefleet, look Dutch too, with their dyked fields, vestigial windmills, old red-brick cottages, rich flower gardens and red-tiled barns. I came alongside the great embankment, hugging the bend of the river, as far as Swinefleet—probably Sweynesfleet, a Danish place this, where less peaceful incomers went ashore—and then struck south and into the marshlands.

Wind had me at its mercy now, blowing strong across Goole Moors and Thorne Waste from south-west or south. A new road was being finished, straight, level, broad and, of course, hedgeless: I buckled down in bottom gear. The daffodil buds and almond blossom of Eastoft passed, still in Yorkshire—just; the road became eel-like, with every wriggle angled more directly into the wind. There was the occasional copse or poplar screen of farm walls, but by Crowle I was ready to make the excuse for a halt, an early cup of tea.

Crowle (pronounced Crool) whose twisting street has too many empty shops, decided otherwise. First I could not locate a café in the sombre little market square, relieved only by the clown-like face of the Grand Dance Hall. When I did find an inconspicuous TEA SERVED UNTIL FOUR door-sign, the tea-room had closed early. Everybody seemed to be out at the old Regal Cinema, converted for the weekend into a motor museum and with all Crowle crammed into its faded foyer. Only 'choc-ices' here.

My unwilling wheel turned towards the next township of the Isle of Axholme, that hermetic inland island of dykes, ditches, canals, eels, water birds and windmills. The wind had now all Hatfield Chase and Hatfield Moors for gathering ground. Single trees along the roadside were 'weeping' like willows under its assault. Gray Green, Bracon, Belton—where a farmhouse recalls the Knights Templar of Temple Bellwood—slowly came and went. At last a slight rise in the uneventful landscape of harlequin-patterned green and brown fields lifted my head to Epworth and its church on the hill. It was the cast-iron saddle, I said to myself, that got me off for the last bit. Then I was pedalling down to the town— and nearly running past it, since it lies off the road and at a right-angle to it.

Cups of tea were definitely *out* here. In the sweets and cigarette shop that was open I learned that all cafés in this Wesleyan Mecca remained shut over Easter. (Perhaps England —or parts of it—does not *want* tourists after all, I thought.) Could I then get bed and breakfast anywhere, I inquired— and, I hoped, thereby achieve grace for a pot of tea too? Well, one pub did catering, the Red Lion, 'You could try.' The Red Lion, facing on to a square with the steps of the village cross from which John Wesley preached, swirling with dust, paper and cartons, was firmly closed on all sides—until opening time. I began to wonder about my chances of bed and breakfast. Should I wait in Epworth nearly an hour and a half or use the time to reach Gainsborough, before dusk, and surely ampler hospitality?

The sun came out: suddenly the sky cleared to brilliant blue: the white-washed cottages dazzled, the red brick façades of houses, banks and pubs glowed. Bright barred shadows of lime trees invited me up the slope of Church Walk: from the little eminence there were views over the whole horizonless countryside. I turned into the church, St Andrews, whose rector for thirty years was Samuel Wesley and whose fabric has not much altered since his time. Evensong was just beginning, a handful of congregation were gathered: the choir entered, the rector's precise voice started the service . . . When it was over I looked in the churchyard, on the south side of the chancel, for the flat table tomb under which Samuel rests. Mounted upon it his son John, providentially saved at six years old from the mob-kindled fire which burned down the old rectory, preached also nightly to crowds, being denied use of the pulpit within the church. (The 'old rectory', in Rectory Street, belonging now to the Methodist Church, a brown brick building of seven not quite rectangular bays and half-hipped roof, is *not* the actual building in which John Wesley and his brother Charles first saw the light.)

When I returned to the Red Lion its doors stood open and 'Claud', thanks perhaps to a combination lock, still rested against a wall. The landlord, nearly submerged by 'leather boys' and their girls, was uncertain, but his wife, after considering, offered a room 'if you don't mind the discothèque next door'. I'd burned my boats: so that was it. What could she supply for supper? Nothing, really, it appeared, as it was the holiday weekend. But . . . within half an hour tomato soup, fried eggs and chips, bread and butter had appeared before me in the snug and disappeared, while there was still another cup or two of tea in the pot.

On balance I'd had quite a successful day: fine throughout, hardish at times, seldom without interest, productive of experience. Epworth, as the wheel wobbles, is about fifty miles from York. As I passed, not much later, the smoke and gloom of the upper room where plump girls in white blouses were dancing together and long-haired youths talking motor-bike in corners, I did not even wonder if the discothèque would keep me awake.

*   *   *

Breakfast was laid for two. I was joined by a cultivated grey-haired lady whose husband, she told me, had died at Epworth. Each spring she stayed there for a few days and was going to lunch that day with the Rector. One of his stories was of Samuel Wesley, father of nineteen children, 'a tartar', who when he had discovered an unmarried mother in his parish made her walk barefoot up the avenue of Church Walk and all down the aisle to the front pew as a public example. It was

John Wesley who had gone to meet her at the porch afterwards to give her his blessing. We chatted about changing
attitudes, other people's customs, the effects of travel and
about Jericho, whose walls we had both recently seen. She
had just returned from a visit to Japan and was now planning
to go to South Africa to see a brother. That in itself seemed
a change of attitude, as meaningful as any, towards widow-
hood.

My road led on to Haxey, a decayed little market town
of red houses, once capital of the Isle of Axholme (now
Epworth's privilege) to Misterton, Walkeringham, Beckingham and Gainsborough. Under a wide sky with a central bowl
of blue, by black sail-less towers of windmills, past long dykes
and lock cottages on a dreamy reach of the Chesterfield canal
I enjoyed this undisturbed Lincolnshire and Nottinghamshire
borderland before traffic was stirring. The fragment of a cross
on Haxey Green, marking the site of an old fair, is carved
with the arms of Mowbray, exiled Duke of Norfolk of Shakespeare's *Richard the Second*. In the farmland there are traces
of 'strip cultivation'—each strip being $16\frac{1}{2}$ feet wide and
covering half an acre. Haxey Hood or 'throwing the Hood',
a medieval game something like Rugby football, is still played
or was but recently on 6 January, with grand scrimmages
between the neighbouring parish youth. In the long 'carrs'
that stretch down to the Trent and to old ferry crossings, now
disused, in the harmonious knot of cottages about a church
and its elms, as at Walkeringham, England here almost
audibly breathes of her past.

From the sharp turn at Beckingham I had a tail wind,
westerly now, into Gainsborough. Rider and bicycle were getting into rapport: I could use my 92 for once, down the
straight, after the low-gear work of the first day. The bridge
over the Trent and the wharves and warehouses to be seen
from it are as attractive as any aspect of Gainsborough. Many
of the warehouses and the bridge also are of the late
eighteenth-century. Behind them are one or two narrow
cobbled streets of character and occasional Georgian fronts,

but the approaches into town and market place are largely Midland red brick, the factories and houses presenting dreary, forbidding faces with traffic roaring between. No doubt market stalls make all the difference to the look of the centre, itself without much dignity. But, unless he found Old Hall and turned away from such grim exteriors as Marshall's Engineering Works and the decayed Victorian terraces, the casual traveller would be likely to give Gainsborough the go-by, *pace* George Eliot and her *Mill on the Floss*.

Old Hall, on a drab piece of grass among some uninspiring semi's is a Tudor, brick-built, turreted manor-house, with an Elizabethan wing front. After use successively as linen factory, theatre, Corn Exchange, Congregational Chapel, pub, work-shop and block of tenements, in the course of two hundred years, it is being restored and lived in again. Burnt once by the Lancastrians and rebuilt in 1484 in time to entertain Richard III, the long baronial hall itself with its massive oak framing and noble roof, and the adjacent kitchen's enormous fireplaces are perhaps the most impressive survivals of the original fabric. From the top of the embattled, polygonal tower one can follow the Trent's course almost to the Humber.

I turned out of the town, not so populous now as it was in 1900, past the station, the corner junk shops and dubious newsagents, on the Lincoln road, but left it and the river plain at the first opportunity. A 'B' road offered a way through to Lincoln, by Kexby, Willingham, Stow and Till Bridge Lane—the Roman way that linked Littleborough beyond the Trent to Ermine Street on Lincoln Cliff, an attenuated con-tinuation of the Cotswold limestone. I had it practically to myself, rolling round the sharp curves and taking the slight ups and downs like a joyride. It was a first taste of the open, lonely roads of Lincolnshire. Pedalling along in sheer plea-sure I turned an abrupt corner, drew clear of a plantation and, without a hint of anything unusual, entered a French village at the foot of a Norman cathedral. Or so it seemed.

St Mary's, Stow, is one of the earliest parish churches in England and one of the most monumental. It rises fortress-like from among the clustered cottages, partly Anglo-Saxon, partly Norman, cross-shaped and with a great central tower. The vista of thirty-foot-high round-headed arches, framing the later pointed ones at the crossing, and the overall length of 150 feet are as grandly impressive as the exterior. For long, but erroneously, known as the mother church to Lincoln, it dominates the plain as the cathedral does the Cliff skyline. I was impelled to stop and gaze longer at the sheer beauty of stone and the great tower with its flag streaming in the wind —from the parlour of the Cross Keys just over the road.

The pub, said the landlord—and Stow— had once been a favourite venue of cyclists. Few came in nowadays—this lunchtime's only other customer was a fellow publican bewailing the old days, when there was no TV but games and songs in pubs, with a pianist playing all evening for free beer, brought in everybody. They both seemed bewildered, a bit stunned and stranded by time's changes: the generous cut of the sandwiches, the price—only 14p with mild—showed what cyclists and others were missing.

The extent of the view back across Lincolnshire's western lowland, running from the Isle of Axholme in the north to the Vale of Belvoir, was a vast reward for the climb, barely 100 feet, from Till Bridge Lane to Ermine Street. That is another of the flat counties' gifts to the cyclist, maximum outlook for minimum effort, when a lift in terrain does come. A few cyclists and walkers were out enjoying this ridge prospect; local crowds were at the stock-racing circuit close by; but when I swung down Ermine Street and by Newport Arch— England's only surviving Roman town gateway—and Bailgate into the cathedral precincts it looked as if every man and his girl from outside—Indian, French, American, Dutch, Chinese—was *there*.

Steep Hill, a narrow, cobbled way with a handrail to assist the pedestrian, had its continuous procession to Aaron the Jew's House, Jew's Court and Aaron's House lower down. The former, said to be the oldest inhabited house in England and the oldest stone-built dwelling in Europe, and certainly

looking the part, was named after a rich Jew who died in
1186: the latter belongs also to the twelfth century and may
have been a synagogue. Steep Hill is indeed one of the most
exciting streets in England. Its other houses are timber-
framed with overhangs or half-sunk into the roadway or else
carry giant pilasters in their upper storeys. The intersection
with Michaelgate is especially picturesque and the views
through to the green slopes of Canwick offer bright contrast to
the ugly, grimy streets and factories of nineteenth-century
Lincoln that spread out 'below the hill' in the damp flats by
the Witham. The whole cobbled slope, of course, burgeons
with tea-rooms, boutiques, antique shops (one formerly a
medieval hostelry, the Harlequin Inn), print shops, book
shops and—to be up with the times—a scarcely camouflaged
'porn' shop at the low end.

Disinclined to hold 'Claud' back all the way down and then
to heave again all the way uphill, I sought out a tea-room with
a window place at the top of the street.

'I'll take your bike, if you don't look out', said a young man
jocularly, leaving as I sat down. 'Been wanting a Claud Butler
for years: can't seem to get hold of one here.'

'I don't think you will,' I said, 'it's locked.'

It was just one of the many times that the machine received
appraisal, sometimes with the comment that it would look
better carrying less. I agreed, from the riding aspect, and was
able to remedy that later on. After tea and toast I sauntered
with the crowd downhill, through the Strait to the Stonebow
which marks the site of the southern gate of this former
Roman city, as Newport Arch marks the northern, Ermine
Street bisecting the whole. I then climbed up again to
Michaelgate, by a winding, tree-shaded lane, empty of the
throng and with the towers of the cathedral soaring over the
roofs. Lincoln's three towers are its conspicuous crown,
whether one comes to this 'old, confused, long, uneven, steep
and rugged town', as John Evelyn described it, by the railway approach or down the long straight of Ermine Street
from the Humber, when for mile after mile they seem never

to get any nearer: or, equally, along the lonely Brant road from the south, or, as I had come, from across the western plain. It is one of the great sights of Europe, hypnotising the newcomer's attention like Chartres across the plain of the Beauce.

I perambulated the cathedral on the outside, the grand array of medieval houses and gateways in Minster Yard, knowing that if I got inside the afternoon would be gone. Lincoln demands days of its own: time to linger not only in a cathedral built by Remigius of Fecamp, Normandy, at the same time as his master William the Conqueror was building the castle, but also by Brayford Wharf—the Swan Pool—which gave Lincoln (Lindum Colonia) its Celtic name Llyndon, and by Water Lane and High Bridge with its unique row of timber-framed sixteenth-century shops and houses; among the many unpublicised churches and chapels; in the Usher Gallery with its paintings of the city by Peter de Wint and Turner; and among the inns, from the old Saracen's Head to the Dickensian White Hart so like a discreet gentleman's club.

Loth, I turned back to 'Claud', skirted the castle walls by Eastgate and sought the Wragby road. At the first turn off I took to the lanes again. Cherry Willingham, Fiskerton, Benedictine Bardney offered their fresh spring gardens, flowering currant hedges, pale green-clothed dykes, nigger-brown ploughland and black-faced sheep, a quiet countryside given style by the creamy-white or strawberry pink campaniles of its village churches, a Yugoslavian touch. From Fiskerton I had the retrospective cathedral view that was de Wint's favourite. Bucknall, Horsington, Stixwould—waterfowl and white violets along the ditches, a westering sun to highlight the white gable ends of farms. Then, dreaming along, as the cyclist does towards day's end, I was suddenly plunged into the gloom of a long coniferous avenue and thick rhododendron coverts, an unexpected wooded island among the delphs and dykes. At the end of it, modern villas and half-timbered hotels, and a surprising sign: THE TEAHOUSE IN THE

WOODS: THE KINEMA IN THE WOODS: THE RHEUMATIC CLINIC. I came out of dreamland to find myself at the centre of Woodhall Spa.

It looked at first as if I ought to have gone for the inn at Bardney, where I had noticed an ACCOMMODATION sign. Woodhall Spa was not going to be easy to crack. The spa hydros, one of them an immense, low, timbered building, full of luxurious Edwardian furniture, and the Golf Hotel, at £4.50 or more, were out of the question, even if they had wanted a cyclist. The pubs, such as there were here, didn't bother with bed and breakfast.

'All too toffee-nosed,' said an off-duty hotel porter, 'and they don't let *anyone* in the bars either. No leather-jackets and jeans and no "pop". Aping Harrogate, they are. You can't build yourself a house here unless it's up to class—£7,000–£8,000. As for keeping a shop, just talk to anyone that does about rates.'

I prospected the outskirts for a bed-and-breakfast sign on some less well-found villa, without result, then, just before it closed, called at a café. Perhaps I'd better have my evening meal at all events. Some other overnight idea might come up afterwards. The proprietor of Lime Tree Café was sympathetic: he knew the problem. Although he did not live in Woodhall himself—going home each evening except in busy times—he had a pied-à-terre over the kitchens. I was welcome, he said, to the spare bed, if I did not mind caretaking for the night. It was the perfect answer. So, after dark, I found myself virtual custodian, from an elevated position on the Broadway, of the whole kursaal.

Woodhall Spa's atmosphere is unusual. When you are there you are subtly taken in by it; once you have left it you could easily put the whole place down to hallucination. First there is the odd enclave itself, like a bit of Surrey, of 'blown sand', heather, conifers, silver birches and rhododendrons, at the end of the clay vale. A single-track railway line, its metals rusting with disuse, running forlornly across the fen away to Boston and up to the wolds at Horncastle, separates the Broadway from a wilderness of tall pines and sandy walks. As I strolled along after supper, under the dark leafy canopy, with the last rays of sun filtering red-gold through the great trunks, the KINEMA IN THE WOODS appeared—a sort of glorified, wooden village hall with fairy lights. 'Tired?, Bored? Lonely? Here is the Remedy. Film entertainment that is different: by modern Back Projection which avoids Flicker on the Screen with No Light Rays in the Hall so that the Picture can be viewed comfortably near the Screen like a Theatre's Stage Play.'

The Kinema was celebrating its fiftieth anniversary: the manager, who I suspect had been there right from the beginning, told me it was not affected by power cuts, since it possessed its own generator. So patrons could always look forward in confidence to their coming entertainment. Moreover, since there was one price of admission only, they could always come in when they chose and sit anywhere they liked. No doubt such facilities had helped many of those seeking their cure. As I moved off towards the TEA HOUSE and the RHEUMATISM CLINIC AND SPA the 'sound of music' followed me from the foyer out among the redwood giants. Just inside the Kinema boundary there are *Sequoia wellingtonia, Sequoia gigantea,* and in the mixed woodlands further on red squirrels and a wide variety of birds, including willow warblers, waxwings, green and spotted woodpeckers and, on occasions, nightingales.

A boys' boarding school, a golf course, a swimming pool and a rose-pergola'd park help to counter the absence of impressive buildings in Woodhall's centre. It seemed empty of life, its hotels and bigger houses retreating within their own grounds, its nucleus of shops soon giving way to one-storey premises on the outskirts, its Victorian churches aloof at either end of the tree-lined street, its crossroads conspicuously free of traffic. The air of 'rural simplicity and rest' was altogether too convincing, too soporific. As I got away after a latish breakfast few doors had yet opened, a steady drizzle was falling: once past the last trees and pedalling down the Tattershall road I began to wonder if such a place really existed.

My equipment included a lightweight waterproof cape and sou'wester, but I was fortunate enough to meet no conditions requiring them. A loosely fitting jacket of double Grenfell cloth and a folding proofed cap proved enough for all weathers. In them now I rode out the hour or so of rain and found even my tweed 'plusses' shedding most of it and soon drying. It was a big advantage to meet showers and winds without being caped up.

Tattershall's huge, menacing red-brick castle keep, built by Lord Cromwell, Henry VI's Treasurer, was just off-route and obscured in the rain, but Coningsby's equally famous fen landmark, the great one-handed clock with its gaily coloured dial of 16½-foot diameter on the church tower, loomed moonily up through the murk. The dial is so large that it was possible to read the time to within five minutes just by the position of the single hand. At New York, a little beyond Coningsby, the road direction veered, the rain ceased and as I came into the long straight stretch across Wildmore Fen wind got up, practically against me, of course.

'You've a lovely bike there,' observed an old labourer as I was consulting the map at Langriville for a way that would avoid it, 'wish it had been mine at eighteen. All these fields had hedges then and us cyclists could use cover in wind. You could get to Boston or where you liked under 'em. Now there's none at all: it's all factory farms everywhere. In another ten years there'll be nothing but diesels on these roads, head to tail.'

And, as I asked him the best way to Boston, he added: 'You might go a bit longer round, but you'll finish not so wet here' (under the arms).

The 'back way' that he had suggested wriggled along close to the river Witham, with the pierced lantern tower of Boston Stump as guide-post. There was an occasional windbreak under the embankment and I could look about me. 'Farmer's pride' was much in evidence, not the old brightly painted wains, but rows of daffodils planted along field borders. The dykes had fat clumps of primroses and white violets. Every so

Page 35 (above) Lincoln, showing its cathedral standing high above the city; *(below)* Boston, Lincolnshire, with the town bridge and the tower of St Botolph (Boston Stump)

Page 36 (above) 'The Brinks' at Wisbech where many handsome Georgian houses overlook the river Nene; (below) a Fenland road

often there was blown across the road the sharp fresh scent of narcissi and daffodil fields in first bloom and at gateways I looked out to a great patchwork quilt, yellow, white, green and brown. Dog Dyke, Gipsy Bridge, Fishtoft Drove tempted the signs, but I steered course by the Stump and suddenly, surprisingly, was in among allotment gardens, aviaries, a back lane, a narrow street, traffic signs. A time-trial cyclist in black tights, cornering at speed, nodded a welcome and then, dismounting, I was in Boston market-place under the statue of Herbert Ingram, founder of the *Illustrated London News*.

The Falcon, tucked in just behind the Stump—and popular with typists and their boyfriends—set me up with sandwiches and shandy. I was soon out again in bright sunlight to enjoy the triangular 'square' spreading under that 272-foot-high tower and octagon lantern, 'the most prodigious of English parochial steeples' (Pevsner). From its leads the square is only a tea-cloth: almost a third of the county of Lincolnshire can be seen and Hunstanton across the width of the Wash. More graceful than the tower of Bruges, it rears on the very edge of the Witham, the source of Boston's' wealth, while the chancel asserts its presence cheek-by-jowl with the coloured awnings of the market stalls. There are marks low down on the west wall showing the level of record high tides. Stone groining within the tower occurs 137 feet above the floor; there are three stages lighted by great windows, the eight-light west window being one of the largest in England. Panelled buttresses climb in steps to the delicately carved parapet with its turret pinnacles from which spring pairs of flying buttresses to support the lantern, formerly a beacon for sailors entering the port. I found the best viewpoint at the other end, the south, of the market-place and from the adjacent Town Bridge, near the Assembly Rooms, where this stupendous Stump—so called because later addition of a spire was contemplated—soars up almost from water level.

Boston is a town for all seasons, and with architectural interest of every period. I was drawn to Spain Lane with its thirteenth-century remains of a Dominican Friary and the cobbled alley of Spain Court, nucleus of Pilgrim College; to South Square with its eighteenth-century warehouses and house of Jean Ingelow, poetess celebrant of the great flood by which Boston was devastated in 1571; by Still Lane to Pump Square, centre of a labyrinth of little streets and brick and timber buildings; to Church House at the corner of Wormgate, Dutch-gabled and motley-tiled, given to the town by Mary Tudor; to old Pescod House in Mitre Lane, off Bargate, the home of a fourteenth-century merchant prince. The mixture is heady: even the neat, brick eighteenth-century terraces have their special décor and their 'floodsteps'. Equally for *Mayflower* descendants and for touring cyclists Boston is a town worthy of repeated pilgrimage. After a final sampling —the Maud Foster five-sail tower mill (1809), still in working order, with its ogee cap—I pulled away, conscious of more riches missed, by the Spalding road,

Again, as on nearly all main routes, I was off it and on a by-road as soon as might be. The field road from Kirton to Fosdyke promised to cut a corner off. After inveigling me along among the unfenced cabbage and daffodil fields, past isolated farms with wildly barking, plunging dogs, into the heart of nowhere, it also gave me a taste of Wash weather. A sudden fierce squall gathered in the region of the Skalp, rain sheeted down, lashing horizontally across the bare road and turning the verges to running mud. It had me scuttling for shelter into a huge, hangar-like storage shed, where a sign read 'Onions 15p stone'. I fortified myself with a few dates from my reserve ration and was on the point of donning sou'wester and cape, but even before they could be unstrapped the storm subsided. The black canopy was lifted and within minutes a washed-blue sky appeared, to make almost luminous the pea-green fields, brown soil and aubretia borders of wayside cottages. Sudden sea-changes add to the charm of these open eastern counties.

Before crossing the Welland, distinctly nautical here in its installations, I drew up at a caravan snack-bar. The owner was proud of his 'conversion', all done by himself to his own design: young and keen and made redundant at his previous maintenance job, he had decided to strike out for himself instead of waiting for labour exchange redeployment. There seemed to be the likelihood of good trade on this major road, linking Kings Lynn to the A1. So far, though, he had waited —and hoped. There had been no callers of any kind for the first two and a half hours of Easter Tuesday: then a trickle only. By way of encouragement I repeated my order, enjoying two freshly made cups of tea and two tarts for 10p. As he went on to tell me, his father had just visited Holland and had found English spring flowers on sale there earlier than the Dutch. Growers in this English 'Holland' had high hopes of the Common Market, he felt his turn might also come.

Except for one thing I should have gone on to Kings Lynn myself: 'Sea-Link' 32-ton box-car trailer lorries were going there too. These 'long vehicles', cruising fast down the A17, with their powerful suction, their dangerous swing and their fumes left little joy for the cyclist, forced to the very edge for safety and then at hazard from sunken drainage grids, them-selves obscured by the downpour's temporary flood. I endured across Whaplode Marsh, but at Holbeach Clough decided that 'Lynn first and safety last' was not the best policy for a round-England tourist. Holbeach instead of Lynn would do for the night—not perhaps so consequential a town, but with a quieter charm of its own. The simple cross-pattern of the streets, as I came in, the fat-budded chestnut trees and paved walks, the early Victorian brick cottages and few Georgian houses, gathered by the tower and tall plain spire of the church into a harmony, seemed to confirm my choice. In the churchyard, as I noted later on, there was a splendid fern-leaf or 'cut-leaf' beech and also a catalpa, one of that ornamental, sub-tropical species—sometimes called the Indian bean— whose large heart-shaped leaves give the deepest shade.

The first pub in the High Street displayed a CTC sign. I went in. 'What does that mean?' asked the landlord with black eye-patch, looking up from a glass with his cronies. 'Cyclists Touring Club—never heard of it. Oh, well, seeing you're one of them,' with a disparaging look at my 'plusses', 'you can have bed and breakfast for —.' He named an amount only 25p less than my daily budget. Saying that I'd be back if I were not suited elsewhere, I went on to the end of the town. The Black Bull was under new management: it offered genuine welcome and subsequently punctilious service, a generous menu, and provided for all my needs, bath, dinner and wine included, at an amount less than the first inn's B & B offer. Part of touring enjoyment is in the night's accommodation: in choosing it, as I was to prove more than once, it pays not to be in too much of a hurry.

A pre-dinner stroll revealed other facets of Holbeach. In West End I came upon Stukeley Hall, too 'fen-mannered' architecturally, but the site of the family home of William Stukeley, one of the founders of the Society of Antiquaries. Serpentine House, of unusual name, was more pleasing to the eye, with its elegant columned porch, curving flight of steps and Regency cast-iron verandah. By way of Victoriana there was an odd cemetery chapel, really two chapels separated by a spire built over an archway, a classical workhouse-turned-hospital and almshouses in the High Street given interest as a group by their central gable. It seemed to add up to a discreet and tasteful little market town of the undisturbed, unexceptional kind that helps to make Lincolnshire a 'county of infinite charm'. Was it? When I called at a stationer's for a view card and remarked something to that effect, his reply 'Well, ye-es, it looks so' cast doubt. Presently he added: 'There's a swapping group, they tell me: wife-swapping, I mean. This Lib. and Love stuff has got everywhere.' And he was in no way abashed to admit, far and away his best-selling line was some of the 'hot stuff'—'real rough' he said—kept for customers of all sorts under the counter.

* * *

Next morning I looked in at Long Sutton and the Easter flower display in its church. A couple from Winchester, making almost a tour of churches in this area—where they could hardly go wrong—had enthused about it at dinner. Both the thirteenth-century tower and the lead spire of the church— the latter feature one of England's earliest—as well as the flowers within were well worth a halt. John of Gaunt had once owned the manor here and the Red Rose of Lancaster could be seen in old glass in the aisle. The little market-place in which the church stands is mercifully set back from the A17, making it pleasant to loiter in. There is a good eighteenth-century building of three storeys and fluted pilasters above. In the window of an antique shop I noticed the biggest collection of old oil table lamps that I've come across —many with highly decorated fonts, with game birds and beasts painted on pale green glass. In comparison with the northern, scruffier Lincolnshire and such places as Crowle or Epworth, the kempt, prosperous Holland division and its towns are altogether rewarding.

Long-vehicle traffic on the Washway still deterred me from lighting out to Lynn. So I turned off south into the fields of daffodils and narcissi, the currant and cider apple orchards, towards Wisbech. A derelict tower mill with six sails stood gauntly against the blue, wind-wracked skies. At tidy Tydd St Mary a sign pointed to the Roman road and if I'd looked for it there were parts of the Roman bank, built to keep out the waters of the North Sea. Wide dykes, seemingly stretching to infinity, dominated the landscape. Then, as I crossed a bridge, a greater waterway appeared, the Nene, and wharves and Rhein cargo boats. This heralded Wisbech itself.

As a town it is a bit mixed up. Capital of the Fens and twinned with Arles-sur-Rhône, it lies in Cambridgeshire, but associates with Spalding on the other side of the Bedford Level in Lincolnshire. Like Spalding, whose houses along the banks of the Welland give it character, Wisbech from the town bridge over the Nene offers North Brink and South Brink. Their rows of merchants' houses are reminiscent of Delft. Behind this dignified waterfront the main part of the town appears nondescript. I might, had the morning been calm and the miles ahead easy, have sought out Peek-over House for its gardens and especially for its maidenhair tree, a 'living fossil' as Darwin called it. This unique tree, the only living representative of its family and known chiefly from specimens at Kew and other botanic gardens, has persisted for about ten million years without any evolutionary change and has also great ornamental beauty. But the morning was far from calm, and riding time could not be squandered.

As I pushed out again to Friday Bridge and into the fen, wind brought my wheels more than once to a standstill. Once beyond Elm—a delightful cluster of pink-washed cottages and pink almond blossom framing a squat, stone church —there was no cover from its buffeting. When the roadway was raised as a causeway over the levels and, with one of its frequent right-angled turns, brought me into the eye of the wind, there was little point in riding. Walking was a better way of making progress and of remustering for the next 'leg'. I was glad of the railway, later on, for its slight protection and not surprised, on reaching March, that it was already late lunch-time.

A street market enlivened this run-of-the-mill, yellow-brick railway town. NO VAN DWELLERS was the sign on most of the pubs: one or two vagrants were loitering in a corner of the square by the Nene. In most parts nowadays they're as scarce as flies in winter. Only at the third place of asking was I able to get a ham sandwich with my beer. But March has at least one notable feature: it provides a council cycle park. 'Yes,' said my neighbour at the bar, 'even the bank manager goes to work on a bike.' He had been a club member, in his time, at first in the fast, racing section, then in the medium, finishing off in the 'social' section. He remembered the 'Glad-it's-over' feeling of the first low gear 25's of the season, run in March or early April. One of his greatest pleasures, he said, had been to watch track racing at Herne Hill, 'the best sport of 'em all'.

Wind, wind, wind all the way to Wimblington, Doddington, Benwick still beside the Nene. In walking 'rests' between
head-down struggles against the 'scourge', I enjoyed seeing
the lively paintwork of cottages—lilac and white, or primrose
and orange doors and window-frames: the pairs of mallard
duck in almost every 'drain', the flight of geese against
scalloped cloud, the black silhouettes of low-flying aircraft.
Farms offered onions now at 10p a stone from these bountiful
fields north of the Forty Foot Drain. When I crossed it, at
Wells Bridge, the worst was over. Beyond this great waterway linking the Nene with the Old Bedford river, the road
switches course. Broad turf verges, blue and red hyacinth
borders to cottage plots, then a screen of trees and the beginning of built-up streets, not all dirty yellow brick this time,
the spacious green before a great church—Ramsey. Only
about forty miles, but I was ready to let the saddle, unaccountably iron-hard again, have a rest.

The Three Horseshoes in Little Whyte—somehow the
whole place recalled those illustrations by Randolph Calde-
cott to the tale of John Gilpin—was changing hands, but
'obliged'. Like Ramsey it had that 'lost-in-the-fen' atmosphere, not unfriendly, but casual where appearances don't
matter. I had a back room looking out on to a dismal back-
yard, the attentions of a roaming bitch on heat, a meal in the
sole company of a 'rep' who never spoke and, later, the offer
of TV in the family lounge with the ailing son of the house.
The pub belonged to the 'Pint and Platter' organisation and
obviously paid its way, if it did, on the pints.

Ramsey could have been depressing. The heavy-browed,
heavy-jowled, all teeth-and-sideburns rural wedding-groups
in the photographer's window shared the 'lost-in-the-fen'
look. The shops were closed, the club near the blue-and-
white painted Wesleyan chapel wasn't opening, the one
cinema was showing some weird, dated and sanguinary
horror film, the wide market-place ran out of interest with
a dreary Railway Hotel, but it *was* out of the wind.

First hour in the morning, last hour in the evening are

usually the best of the cyclist's day: one has verve, the other a mellowness of *fait-presque-accompli*. After overnight rain the morning sparkled as only fen mornings can; skies were scoured, horizons etched, colours brilliant. It was a pay-off day, too, on the score of wind. With tail or side winds I could romp away out of Ramsay Hollow and up to Warboys, Fenton, Pidley, St Ives without effort—on a road which Virginia Woolf, as a girl of seventeen, used to cycle when staying at Warboys Rectory. Warboys still had more than passing interest: a fleet, some dozen or more, of vintage Rolls Royce and Bentley limousines, with immaculately restored coachwork up to fifty years old, stood in parade order on a carriage sweep just off the crossroads. Beyond, the road's swinging curves and undulations, the wide coloured prospect in fresh greens, browns and boundless overhead blue, exhilarated.* A cursory look at Oliver Cromwell, St Ives' statued son in the market-place, and a lingering one at the lovely swan-haunted medieval bridge over the Ouse, complete with its tiny chapel, and I was off again for Needleworth and the Over Ferry.

The Overcote Inn was there—and the Pike and Eel—but, in spite of the assurance of a St Ives traffic warden that the ferry still operated, it had not done so, said a fisherman, for three years. 'At Over they fling oaths at me,' I muttered and wondered how many of the old river ferries *are* still in use in England? My by-road way to Cambridge was blocked. So to Bluntisham and Earith, still under resplendent skies, where The Crown offered snack lunches.

I took my lunch out to the riverside garden, to one of the white-painted iron tables set among weeping willows and double-almond trees. There was an upturned dinghy against a plum tree, borders of wallflowers, tulips, primula and daffodils; there was sunglow on the ochre-washed walls and russety-yellow pantiles of an outbuilding, the sound of water cockling against a mooring-stage and a parade of swans with

---

* 'Coming back we forgot all our cares—in gazing—absorbing—sinking into—the sky. You don't see the sky until you live here.'—Virginia Woolf

their cygnets. Memories of Mr Polly at the Potwell Inn...
Down-wind came a trio of swans in flight almost translucent
against the sun. It deserved another half of Watney's mild,
another few minutes to bask and savour the joys of touring.
'Thought you'd have been in Lynn by now' joked the landlord as I went in with my glass.

I was pushed along now by Ouse Fen, close beside the Old
West River with views across rippled water and wind-waved
tall grasses to Haddenham on its hill, towards Willingham,
Long Stanton, Oakington and Girton. Cherry orchards and
Chivers jam country this, resplendent, no doubt, in a few
weeks' time with snowy clouds of blossom. At Girton I joined
the Via Devana, the A604, and was swept with the rush of
traffic past the red-brick college portals pell-mell over Magdalen Bridge into Cambridge.

Crocodiles of tourists, Continental, Indian, American,
Chinese—the Chinese student crops up everywhere at all
seasons, equally avid, it seems, of contact with the British
cultural heritage whether at Wells Cathedral or Wordsworth's
cottage. They filed along the narrow ageless street (bear-led
by their appointed guide), past the famous escutcheoned gateways, peering into Trinity Great Court, oblivious of Caius,
anxious to see the Bridge of Sighs. Leaving 'Claud' in a
passageway, I stepped into a famous and familiar old bookshop—not the ubiquitous Heffers—to avoid the hurly-burly,
and went unrecognised in my Pakistani beret and plus two's.
The steps of all sightseers lead to King's and the chapel,
unkindly likened to a farrowing sow recumbent, that ranks
among the great buildings of Europe. The crocodile was
there also, drinking in the immaculate lawns and cobbled
walks, the mellow texture of stone and green-bronze fountain,
the brightly coloured and gilded shields, the assured, spacious
planning of a college founded in 1441 and at first the exclusive preserve of Etonians.

The market-place, just off King's Parade and in the heart
of Cambridge, has not yet been overtaken by one of the stereotyped schemes for converting open into closed markets, so

often destructive of a town's individuality whether at Birmingham, Barrow or Burnley. Its stalls and awnings, its mixture of fish and vegetables, flowers and fruit, of Indian cottons and David's old books, provides the brashness and bustle of everyday life to offset Senate House dignity, academic reserve and the world of exclusive tailordom. Cambridge gathers 'town' and 'gown' together here, and in Petty Cury and the backways about the Corn Exchange and theatre.

I walked across King's bridge and down the long avenue, palely purple with its last crocuses, to glimpse the especial distinction of Cambridge—the 'Backs', uniquely beautiful association of fine trees, unforgettable buildings and willow-hung river. Then by Queen's for another look at Newton's Bridge and Erasmus' Walk, past Catherine's and Pembroke to my own college. The porter, no longer top-hatted, dozed in his lodge. I had toyed with the idea of claiming an entitled dinner in hall and perhaps spending a night within college walls, if there was a gown to lend and a room free.

'No, Sir: no 'all now, except in term time, Sir. Nearly all the Fellows is away and there is no 'igh table. Whether there may be a room I couldn't rightly say, Sir. You could ask the Secretary up——staircase.' But what is a night in college except in the aftermath of dinner, and that from a kitchen once reputed to be the best in the University? I left the porter to his doze and walked back to my bicycle.

The London road, the A10, out of Cambridge is like any other trunk road—after passing the Fitzwilliam Museum, Addenbrook's Hospital and the Botanical Gardens—a dizzying whirl of traffic. Just beyond Trumpington, where 'worse than oaths were flung at one', according to Rupert Brooke, I left it. By quieter ways amongst arable and woodland burnished by late sun, climbing and dipping gently, I came to Fowlmere. Should I go on to Royston and the A10 again, for my night's accommodation? No: it was almost certain to be noisy, and

Royston men in the far South
Are black and fierce and strange of mouth.

Samuel Pepys had stayed once, in 1675, at the Chequers in Fowlmere: the Black Horse opposite had a CTC sign. I'd try the club recommendation first.

The pub was not yet open, but in due course, at my repeated knock, the landlady came to the back door, straightening her hair after a nap. No beds, sorry, and nothing much in the way of meals, she said, but if I'd care for a caravan berth down the garden, I was welcome, and she'd set it to rights. She did, with clean sheets, warm water in a can and tooth-cleaning water in a cut glass decanter. Not much later I was being handed soup, sausage and mash, cheese, an apple and beer over the bar, while a log fire blazed under the canopy of the wide inglenook.

The Black Horse had few evening callers, apart from a fellow publican's family. WORK IS THE CURSE OF THE DRINKING CLASSES read a motto over the bar—but the position, it seemed, had altered. 'The farm labourer can't afford to visit a pub nowadays,' said one of the few customers. 'You put down a pound note and come out with nothing in an hour.' Fowlmere with a population of about 400 had once supported five pubs. There are three today, but a large syndicate restaurant was going up on a corner site—for Newmarket racegoers. With this and all the other building and pulling down in the last five years the face of the village would soon be completely changed. Recently land had been sold for 140 new houses, a dormitory for Cambridge. Those in the bar didn't like it, but what could you do? This pub might be the next to go, when the present tenants retired.

Soon then, as in many other places within reach of a motorway, earmarked for 'overspill' or commutable for the metropolis, only the 700-year-old church, with its shining flintwork, mini-spire and cerulean clock face, would be left of the old known landmarks that made up for the locals, as here in Fowlmere, *their* village.

CHAPTER TWO

SOUTHERN AIRS

Riding against the wind requires some definite object to urge one on, and that object is best obtained when home is the goal; then the wind may die out.

IN a sense London begins at Cambridge, with metropolitan manners and entertainments, types of hotel, shop and restaurant, flat-converted yellow-brick terraces and potentially commuting traffic. In somewhat the same way, I felt, after leaving Fowlmere, to be leaving the eastern counties and entering the sphere of the south. Not straight away, perhaps, but certainly by the end of another day's ride out of this still rural-mannered village and into groomed and tittivated, tourist-conscious places like Woburn. It was a subtle change of atmosphere which was to persist and strengthen as I left Bedfordshire and Bucks for Berkshire and Hants, and was in stronger contrast still to the 'goneness' of Lincolnshire.

A brilliant early morning after more overnight rain had my wheel on the road betimes. I cut across the A 10 to Meldreth where the thatched cottages were painted Cambridge blue and white, where the Methodist chapel was up for sale and where university affluence could be assumed in the neo-Georgian houses and stylishly converted watermill. Hedges were back now, a welcome feature, high and white with blossom, while in the ditches were white and blue violets. I missed out Shepreth, swinging south-west for Kneesworth and Bassingham just across the A 14.

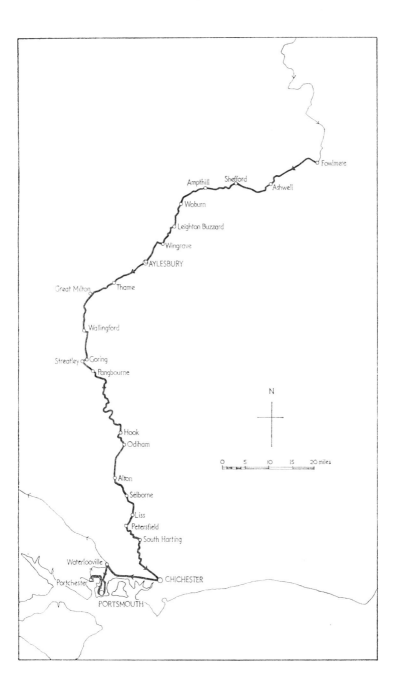

Fowlmere

Ampthill Shefford Ashwell

Woburn

Leighton Buzzard

Wingrave

AYLESBURY

Great Milton Thame

Wallingford

Streatley Goring
Pangbourne

Hook
Odiham

Alton
Selborne

Liss
Petersfield
South Harting

Waterlooville
Portchester CHICHESTER
PORTSMOUTH

N

0   5   10   15   20 miles

A short but heavy shower dismounted me for shelter under the overhanging hedge. I was joined shortly by a passer-by, for whom the sight of my Claud Butler opened memory's floodgates. He had once belonged to Edmonton CC and the 'Century Club'—entry qualification, 100 miles of road within five hours. Later he had joined a 'Loiterers' Club', for week-end outings to places like Blenheim and for holiday tours. They'd had lantern lectures at Sadler's Wells by a celebrated cyclist who always brought along evening clothes in his saddle bag, and an annual dinner with ninety or more present at an Epping Hotel. Cycling then was done in style: when the club had been touring in Ireland commissionaires at the hotels had always taken over their machines to stow them safely for the night. Of course there was not the traffic at home either then: when the rare car did come along, on one of those quiet roads, the club steward at the rear shouted 'Oil'. And the granite chips on the side roads were of different colours, so you always knew which county you were in. Glorious days!

The rain cleared. On to Litlington, Steeple Morden, Ashwell-of-the-Seven-Springs. Cottages now were weather-boarded or timber-framed in diamond designs, walls decorated with plaster trowel-work. A landscape almost Persian in extent and uniformity drew the eye over vast undulating fields of sandy soil, not unlike desert, to distant pencils of spires—minarets—against vague illimitable horizons. Occasionally a turfy lane held encampments of gipsies, the local Bedouin. After so much of 'Holland' and the flat fenland it was a pleasant change to switchback up and down these gentle contours.

At Ashwell the Rose and Crown was just opening its doors. While I enjoyed my mid-day ham sandwich the Cockney landlord discoursed of living in a village, one with some former repute as a cure centre for its mineral springs and still remarkable for some of its old buildings, but quiet indeed after his native Paddington. He wouldn't go back there now and to all the frenzied rush, even for a holiday.

Trade was not spectacular but steady enough to live on and here he could really enjoy his time off. Not, of course, as he once had done in cycling out to Runnymede, but in his garden or the green countryside. He thought his father who had served with the Cyclist Rifle Corps and been wounded in 1916 would have lived much longer if he could have quit the 'smoke' . . .

This leisurely cross-country route came to an end soon after Newnham when it met the A1. From there I took the direct route to Strefford, Clophill, Ampthill, Woburn, chiefly in order to achieve position for striking south without getting toiled in the tentacles of London. The whish, whish, whish of the A1 passed overhead, Strefford put out no lures, rain fell but woodland protected me on the way to Clophill. It had freshened the daffodil and narcissus borders of the orchard garth and the mill pool that grace the old mill there, devoted now to antiques—TRADE AND SPECIFIC ENQUIRIES ONLY. Shortly after, with the A6 also safely behind me, I drew up in Ampthill, Bedfordshire.

A dignified group of seventeenth-century almshouses and church, enclaved just off the approach hill, set the town's tone. The obelisk pump at the crossroads is dated 1784: in Woburn Street, just behind the parking space, Catherine Cross (1773) commemorates Catherine of Aragon's stay there, during her divorce. The importance of Ampthill's coaching era is recalled by hotels like the White Hart and other Georgian premises with tall dignified fronts and sash windows, pillared porticoes and arched yard entrances. There is a Moot Hall and some good houses of chequer brick-work and distinctive door hoods: one, with a fine classic door and pillared porch is by Henry Holland. A modest showpiece, in fact, only marred by the snarl of traffic round the cross-roads and the heavy lorries constantly rumbling through between Bedford and the M1.

I sought a temporary island of quiet in the Coffee House, a cottage shop where a request for more hot water for my cup of strong tea brought an extra cup without charge. 'We all know that cycling's thirsty work' said the smile that accompanied it.

Just outside the town, on the road to Woburn, I passed through a double avenue of limes, planted by Lady Holland and called the 'Alameda' in imitation of a famous avenue in Madrid. The last miles of the road, unless one cuts through the Park, for a glimpse of the egrets and velvet-antlered deer, lead one a dance round three angles of the ducal estate wall, then, after a sudden downhill swoop, into town by the back entry. Woburn itself is purely Rex Whistler. Its impeccable façades, glowing red-brick in late sun, rise from the tiny square exactly like a backcloth for the 'Rake's Progress'. The genteel, gleaming glass bow windows, shiny brass knobs and knockers and letter-boxes, the flagged and cobbled walks, trimmed shrubs and ornamental lamps, the rocking-horse rampant over the doorway of an antique shop, the market house and the eighteenth-century rectory, these add up to something more stagey than real. At the end of the street stands the great entrance arch to Woburn Park, to which, in fact the whole town seems but an anteroom. This, however, with the Nature Reserve and Antiques Market, the lake in the grounds and the house remodelled for a former Duke of Bedford by Henry Holland, demands a tour of its own. It would have delighted the editor of *The Rambler*, 1897, who embarked on a series of 'Rides with an Object'—chiefly England's natural and historical treasures—in order to counteract 'too great a tendency among those who use the wheel to regard it as a mere vehicle for conveying the rider at the quickest possible pace, and by the shortest possible route from one place or one hostelry to another'.

To go to a hostelry for the night at Woburn would have been too much like putting up in a shop-window or showcase. I took advantage of the evening sun and pushed on, across the A5 to Heath Reach and Leighton Buzzard. The traffic on the A5 was relentless. At the awkward crossing-place, with the junction road far out of alignment, it nearly trapped and caught me in the middle lane. Everyman's projectile, hurtling

Page 53 (above) King's College, Cambridge; *(below)* St Ives, Huntingdonshire, by the ancient bridge over the river Ouse, with the spire of All Saints' Church in the background

Page 54 (above) Ashwell, Hertfordshire; (below) Church Street, Aylesbury, Buckinghamshire, with its old church and Georgian houses

down the doomway of Watling Street, seemed aimed at destruction, mine or the driver's. Accidents are no deterrent to the frenzy of speed: handling of power blots out reason like a drug. Does it, perhaps, unconsciously provide the illusion that in driving twentieth-century man shares attributes of deity?

Leighton-and-Linslade had obviously interesting features: I promised myself a more leisurely look in the morning. For this day's end, after forty-eight miles, I claimed the always offered hospitality of a friend's house a little further on. There I took the opportunity of leaving, for collection later, sou'wester and cape, and a few other items which had turned out to be not so much necessities as nuisances. One of them was a can of oil; another, inadvertently, my shaving kit.

*   *   *

Although daily mileages mattered on this tour, if I was to complete it within the time available, repeating figures makes tedious reading. For the rest it's enough to say that, when I had more miles 'in my legs', on occasion I rode up to eighty miles in the day, which would have been far too much at the start. A cautionary tale, told by Alec Waugh in *The Balliols* of an earlier age of cycling, has its bearings here:

A friend had presented Balliol with a book in which the cycling enthusiast might enter his runs, the distances and times, the average of miles per hour. Within a very short time the fever of figures had bitten Balliol. He was always out to beat his own record ... He no longer cycled for the pleasure of the open air and open country; for exercise and the sense of speed; the freedom of being away from bricks and pavements. He cycled with one eye on the clock, the other on the cyclometer. He kept saying, 'Now do you think we could reach Shenley within twenty-three and a half minutes?' He grew resentful of wayside rests at the end of a long pull up a hill. He kept taking out his little book, writing

55

figures, comparing figures. At the end of a day instead of talking lazily before a fire, he would draw up charts by means of which he would invariably discover that there was some record or other that he had broken, even if it was no more than the speed record for the first twelve minutes after tea.

In this Edwardian's bicycling his wife could take no pleasure—the carefree spirit had departed, and, not surprisingly, Balliol soon took up golf. It was this spirit, however, that I was most keen to preserve.

Next morning Leighton-with-Linslade, whilst not being in any sense a showpiece, revealed both charm and character. Its triangular centre plan is agreeably unstereotyped. In the market-place it has a fifteenth-century pentagonal market cross, transitional between the stepped and the arched type, and in the High Street its own architectural vernacular of roses and lions in plasterwork as finials to door and window heads. The dignified classical hotel contributes a fine free-standing swan as its sign. A row of early almshouses carries the original plaque and scriptural motto to each, while the GPO still retains its Victorian letter box. The Golden Balls nearby is one of several ancient inns. In its context the dark ironstone of the church is as striking as the entasis of the high spire, which gives the effect of a Buddhist *stupa*. On the west door there are early fourteenth-century wrought-iron hinges. Their elaborate vine-leaf and scroll design almost covers the wooden surface, in a pattern repeated on the grille to the tomb of Eleanor of Castile in Westminster Abbey; both almost certainly having been made by the same craftsman, Thomas de Leghtone. And, like Buckingham, Thame and Amersham, Leighton has one of the surviving street markets in these parts, which does much to enhance its weekend appeal.

Massed thunderclouds and dramatic shafts of sunlight, swirls, veils and blankets of hail and rain, interspersed with skies of great brilliance over the Chilterns, heralded my departure to Aylesbury, *en route* for Thame and the Thames valley. The air was cooler, the sun warmer, wind north-west, a mixture less anti-cycling than some that I had experienced near the Wash. Not wishing to lose my morning in Aylesbury I sampled only the older part near the church and in St Mary's Square behind it. There is Parson's Fee and Pebble Lane with its huge iron stand-pump and the eighteenth-century Prebendal House, associated with John Wilkes the satirist, now a girls' school. After nodding acquaintance with the statues of Disraeli and John Hampden, after admiring the medieval gateway of the King's Head, but failing to find the Dark Lantern inn in a side alley off the main square, I averted my gaze from that monstrous Tower of Babel—'a fine symbol of modern architecture' a well-known guidebook calls it—the County Council offices and struck out for the Oxford road. At the roundabout which was intended to unscramble traffic pouring through to and from London and Birmingham I did my bit to 'keep death off the roads' and walked.

Soon, however, I was off the trunk route and enjoying the peaceful village way to Thame. Haddenham checked my rhythm for a few minutes—a rambling, characterful village with good triangular green and houses with 'witchert' walls to their gardens, a local variant of roofed cob. All too soon this by-lane emerged through the last of 'leafy Bucks' and into the A 418. Fortunately for Thame, traffic is diverted from its immensely wide main street, whose characteristic 'island' buildings of former market encroachment include Town Hall, an inn and several shops. So the dignity of its old inns, the timbered fifteenth-century Birdcage, the tall, spacious Queen Anne Spread Eagle of gastronomic fame, and the gentility of its modern tea-rooms can be savoured comparatively undisturbed. Except, of course, on market or show day, when the bustle of going and coming knows no barriers and the house, facing the market-place, where John Hampden, freedom's champion, died, looks out on Petticoat Lane *in petto*. Market was in full swing when I arrived—the usual flowers, fish, fruit mixed in with old and new clothing, pop records, paperbacks, cheap hardware and cheaper bric-a-brac.

The Lord William's Grammar School, founded by a sixteenth-century lord of the manor, survives at one end of this very English town: both John Hampden and John Milton were at school there. There is also a prebendal of the bishops of Lincoln, recalling times when the diocese of Lincoln reached from Humber to Thames. The town was originally cast of sound metal, but more recently, no doubt, some of the lustre of Oxford's 'golden circle' has rubbed off on Thame as well. With almost a tail wind now I sailed along in top gear over the rolling road between shining fields of plough bounded by views of the blue Chilterns. A land of great houses and choice estates: the nearest was Waddesdon, a Rothschild house built in the style of a French château, with a view that took in four other Rothschild houses—Halton, Tring, Mentmore and Ascott. The sign and lane to Great Milton were attractive and I found myself in a delightful sequestered village of Oxford marmalade-coloured stone with a fine Early English church. From the *Magnolia grandiflora* in the garden of the 'big house' and the estate cottages with their window arches and door tops in alternating red and blue brick, to the 'Lion's Den' in the Old Red Lion inn, it had style and charm. Others apparently thought so too. During my shandy-and-sandwich break the bar filled up—with voices from Oxford.

'Is it possible for a girl to get up the aisle four months pregnant, without anyone noticing?' queried a blonde.

'Sure. Get her surrounded by bridesmaids: 25 per cent do.' Then, blonde to friend of friend:

'Married, are you?'

'Yes'. Hearty laughter.

'Have you got a job yet?'

'No'.

'What happens if you don't?'

'Go on the dole.'

'Oh—shouldn't bother then . . .'

Thunder clouds had gathered again when I set out. The Oxfordshire plough assumed a rich dark plum-cake colour, the great creamy stone square of Newington House had an almost fluorescent background of beeches, a white horse leaned over a gate, a cherry tree wore its white against a sky of navy blue. There was the first empty thrush egg on the grass verge and broken views towards the 'dreaming spires'. The whole afternoon trembled with rain, but none fell except in great sweeps on the Chilterns.

I hastened on past more tempting signs—to Brightwell Baldwin, Britwell Salome, Berrick Prior and Berwick Salome (why Salome?)—on to Stadhampton, Warborough and Wallingford. Stadhampton's pleasant common, crossed by an avenue of lime trees, and Warborough's carefully tended thatch and roadside seats marked it as the desirable commuter's village. Then over the Thames at Shillingford bridge, a three-arched beauty, and to Wallingford, this bottle-neck on the Oxford–Reading, London–Swindon roads, burgeoned with Georgian buildings, well-preserved old inns and expensive antique shops, in which traders sat idle like so many spiders in their cunningly wrought webs.

The great castle of this ancient town, whose name denotes that its ford was a crossing used even before the Romans established a station there, has vanished. Its earthen ramparts formed three sides of a quadrilateral with the river acting as protective boundary on the fourth side and were built by a follower of William the Conqueror. Most of the town lies within these ramparts, which can still be followed. Old narrow streets, whose use is precluded to cars, a spacious market-place with a seventeenth-century Town Hall and the Norman church of St Mary-le-Mere, whose tower was rebuilt in 1653 with materials from the castle, all contribute to its air of antiquity. (In medieval times Wallingford had fifteen churches and chapels but within a hundred years of the Black Death only four were in use.) I enjoyed a saunter about the by-lanes near the square, found a nice copy of *Zuleika Dobson,* Max Beerbohm's Oxford love story, admired the tall open spire of St Peter's church on Thames Street—designed by Mr Justice Blackstone who lies buried there—and then sought out the handsome twenty-arch stone bridge down the hill over the river.

I crossed the bridge in order to enjoy this rich Thames-side country from the quieter side. At first beechwoods and flints, then sculptured Chiltern slopes, light brown with rashes of pebble or quilts of springing corn, led down to watermeadows, fringed with pollarded willows, with now and then a glass-smooth weir. The road cut an exhilarating traverse across the slopes of these bold and lofty chalk hills, giving wide, uninterrupted views and bringing me out to expansive Goring, with its spick-and-span school boathouses and mock-Tudor pubs. A blue and white launch arrowed up the broad bosom of the river, between Goring Lock and Cleve Lock, skirting the islets.

'Not many bed-and-breakfast places hereabouts.' The garage man knew his Pangbourne, favourite of visitors for its combination of woodland and river, home of a nautical college and once of Kenneth *Wind in the Willows* Grahame. I did, in fact, discover one, rather depressed in appearance among the Reading road terraces, but no one came to answer the bell. So instead I came to the Cross Keys, set on a daffodil-fringed trout stream (the Pang) among old black-and-white cottages. The back door at which I knocked was called 'The Keyhole'. 'Claud' went into the garden shed and I went into a double bedroom facing the road. With an oil stove to air it and scalding water from an Ascot heater in the bathroom it cost £2, including breakfast. For evening meal—quite a problem sometimes on tour when pubs are unprepared—I resorted to the 'Mantrap' for soup and roll, chicken and chips in would-be romantic half-darkness. It was no worse and no better than the fare at a tourist-halt in, say, Jallalabad.

✻   ✻   ✻

'I always come here for the food,' said the young commercial at breakfast next morning, as his cereal-and-cream dish was cleared and his two eggs, bacon, tomato, mushroom,

fried bread, coffee, rack of toast and marmalade appeared.
He had taken up freelance space-selling on advertiser's com-
mission for some large group in disgust at his old conditions
as apprentice water-installation draughtsman at Scunthorpe.
'The grass all round that town was dead and brown,' he volun-
teered, 'just like a moonscape.'

But more discouraging had been the dead hand of the
union. Membership was required, a levy—supposed to be
voluntary—was exacted every week in support of workers in
allied unions when 'out', and union representatives, he
insisted, were always trouble-seeking, anti-settlement, power-
conscious. For himself he was happier to be on the road five
days a week and to live within sight of his native moors in
Lancashire, though it was hard on the wife.

After a latish start I steered course to avoid Reading, to
keep clear of Basingstoke and to find country ways into Hampshire. A narrow by-road to Sulham brought me over Beech-
wood Hill—vantage point for views across the Thames valley
—and Tilehurst Common, one of the south-country type of
rough open space encroached upon by the suburban outliers
of Reading. Escape from the thresh of 'long vehicles' and the
road works of the A 4 brought me to the Kennet valley, with
a weir, an old mill (devoted to antiques), weekend boats and
a waterway quiet-moving as a canal.

From there I plunged into that complex of ancient wood-
land and bewildering lanes which has its centre in Silchester:
Calleva Atrebatum, once a grand junction of Roman roads,
with five gates of entry from Londinium, Alchester, Corinum
(Cirencester), Sorbiodunum (Salisbury) and Venta Belgarum
(Winchester). It lies in the triangle between the A 4 and the
A 33. Within a mile or two I was lost, lost to all traffic sounds
and sense of direction, somewhere in the neighbourhood of
Round Oak and Mortimer Common instead of coming out,
as I had intended, to Stratfield Mortimer and Beech Hill.
'The country is lonely and the by-roads very circuitous' says
a Home Counties compendium, 'the motorist should consult
maps when exploring this district.'

Half the trouble was the absence of two or three of its four arms on each rare signpost and the profusion of minor junctions without signposts at all.

'Ah,' said a carrier whom I stopped, 'you are in Squire Benyon's land, all that from here up to Theale. What you want is Duke o' Wellington's, Stratfield Saye and that there beyond.'

Perhaps I did. Instead of penetrating to the remains of the amphitheatre outside Calleva Atrebatum, with the appearance of the crater of some volcano densely overgrown with trees and shrouded in ivy' (Harold Clunn), or to the two-mile circuit of the Roman town walls, built by the father of Constantine the Great, I pressed on towards the Duke's house. Eventually among great estate farms, riding stables and pig-geries, and the occasional brick-and-timbered cottages I found myself emerging to wider views, across the Loddon valley, then to Stratfield Turgis and Turgis Green. A last plunge, across the A33 and into the next maze of lanes, starred with anemones, stitchwort, white violets, and I emerged again—at the Leather Bottle, Mattingley, on the A32. I was ready for my pickle-and-cheese sandwiches and drink at the public bar, while the landlord had a curt exchange with some 'playboys' who had been ordering pints in each other's name for the lounge and then each denying his responsibility to pay. Here, though, my snack was 18p—4p up on Lincolnshire's Stow.

To Hook and Odiham and over to Alton it had to be the A32, but during lunch hour not at its busiest. Helicopters droned overhead, large tracts of flattish, featureless plough-land gave place to deceptively smooth, arduous gradients as the road bisected a fold in the downs through a chalk cutting. Dead pheasants on the roadside were the traffic victims, wher-ever a copse skirted the route. Odiham, to its good fortune, lies off the A32 for the most part. Its main street preserves the architectural decencies, dignity and spaciousness of an earlier age in contrast to Alton, situated athwart the A31, with its medley of cafeteria, 'washeteria', boutiques, Oxfam shops and multiple stores.

I loitered for a while in Odiham, pleasantly situated on the side of its chalky hill. Kings of Wessex had a royal villa here and the remains of a castle, built soon after the Conquest, can be identified in a farmhouse called Palace Gate. Under Edward III David Bruce of Scotland was confined in that castle for eleven years. I was enjoying the Georgian seemliness of houses and inns, one, the George, going back to the sixteenth-century, when a couple of oak chairs placed outside a small shop in a side street attracted attention. It turned out to be the usual mixed secondhand furniture and curio shop, with a few prints that I wanted to examine. The difference was, I found, that the owner had moved to Odiham from Manchester as a wartime evacuee—and was still hoping to go back, when retirement allowed. Ex-metropolis country-dwellers usually told the other tale, but to a Manchester native, it seems, southern airs were a less strong lure, even after a quarter of a century, than the pull of the North.

Alton was no place for an overnight stay—although Edward Gibbon treated his militia company to the famous local ale there. I took a minor road just beyond its outskirts and came, instead, in late benign sun to Gilbert White's Selborne. Cawood (Yorks), Stow (Lincs), Ashwell (Herts), Milton (Oxon), Selborne (Hants), all could be considered 'star' villages in their various ways, but only the last one celebrated —by association with a naturalist's fame. While sun lasted I strolled by Short and Long Lyth into White's woodland, sheltered and still bountiful of violets, woodspurge, primroses, wood sorrel. I walked the three-quarter-mile length of the village street, admiring the cottages built of freestone, set as in crazy paving, the brick-and-timber houses with their espaliers and topiary, the green of Plestor ('play-stow' or 'play-place') about which old shops, bakehouse and church harmoniously gather. There were of course, 'antiques' signs, buttery bars, tea-shoppes and a car park near the 'zig-zag' path, but the overall impression remained of a place which had altered little, and that very gradually, since the time when White was living at The Wakes. The very same trees can be seen in the view from one well-known house as in an eighteenth-century painting of it. The sombre presence of the Hanger, 'vast hill of chalk, rising three hundred feet above the village and divided into a sheep down, the high wood and a long hanging wood altogether beech' (White, *The Natural History of Selborne*) and of the sudden, deep-cut, hidden valleys that give Selborne its identity have had much to do with this feeling of changelessness.

Formerly three-fifths of the royal forest of Wolmer lay within Selborne parish, a particularly extensive one abutting on twelve neighbours. It proved somewhat coy, however, about such mundane matters as bed and breakfast. A lady helper at the Bakehouse, who lived in a cottage down the lane, would perhaps have done it—but just now she was all in a turmoil with decorators: or one of the antique shop owners might oblige, seeing that it was not yet the busy season. Or I might perhaps try at the new tea-rooms. There was always, of course, the AA hotel and its buttery bar— but, then again, if I was touring on a *bicycle* . . .

I tried the tea rooms. The proprietress was still in the enthusiastic stage of 'we try to offer what is asked for at any hour, tea at dinner time, just a pot of coffee during lunch hour or even breakfast up to 3 pm. We don't impose fixed times, we don't cut on quality, we make everything ourselves from the best ingredients, and we rely for our profits on return trade.' With a daughter still at convent school, a son just launched and a husband commuting daily to the City, she was keen to make a go of it with this uncharacteristic customer service. I was given a snug bedroom and an appetising snack menu for supper—a soup, Welsh rarebit and fruit. It was a pleasant change, taken in a tea-room with shelves of books and bibelots—a business sideline.

Whilst I was having supper the husband returned home, and had to be off again next day before seven. Commuting by car, bus, rail from Selborne to London, a two-hour journey, was it worth it? For the time being, perhaps, and with gardening-and-sleep weekends, but the aim was to build up tea-room business and etceteras until he could cut free of office chores altogether and work from home as a freelance writer/editor. The circle of commuterland reaches far enough, south from the metropolis to the coasts of Sussex and Kent, north at least to Luton in Bedfordshire, west to Reading and Haslemere, without imposing its ways of life and attitudes on more village communities. Those who have personal stakes in London, mixing usually work and pleasure, divide their allegiance between the city itself and the place where they live, with inevitable weakening of feeling for the local community and often adherence to standards which create barriers to genuine neighbourliness. Life, my hosts felt, would be freer and more satisfactory if it could be lived in Selborne without this split personality and the drag of double values. *Prosit!*

*   *   *

Benign as Selborne's evening had been, the morning was even milder and sunnier. I turned away from the looming Hanger, negotiated a sudden steep twist of road downhill, cruised along to Liss and was entering Petersfield before that bright-looking market town was fully awake. Once a wool-trade and coaching centre, Petersfield has interesting streets—The Spain, Sheep St, Music Hill—and Georgian buildings enough to merit a perambulation. But the day and the hour were not for halting yet. With a metaphorical bow to the figure in the square of William III in Roman garb, and a backward glance at an outdoor antiquarian books arcade, I was away—past the boating mere and heading for the villages of the South Downs.

The first taste of the real south country: smooth, subtly curved breasts of hills; narrow, high-hedged winding lanes with wild plum, buckthorn and blackthorn in blossom; dense hanging woods of beech and ash; lazily meandering brimstone and peacock butterflies; lush green pastures and light chalky soil; Kiplingesque 'little lost down churches'.

The first village, South Harting, was an obvious addition to my starred list, a very considerable village and highly rated at Domesday. Its Early English church tower with green copper spire is a real eye-catcher: there are stocks and a whipping-post, flint-faced and thatched cottages, views up every lane to the pastel-shaded down skyline. Anthony Trollope lived here: his pen and paperknife are preserved in a showcase within the church.

Resisting the temptation to laze there, with a drink and a seat in the sun. I pushed—literally—up the long, steep, wooded bank behind South Harting to enjoy more extensive downland views. The South Down Way leads off, nearby, at Uppark, itself now a National Trust property. This is the house that a grateful nation sought to offer to the Duke of Wellington, as a gift, after the battle of Waterloo. A gift declined because, he said, he estimated he would need eighteen fresh horses every year to pull his carriage up the hill from South Harting on his way from London—the hill that I had just pushed up. There is a folly tower, circa 1770, in the grounds and within décor and furnishings that have not been changed since the eighteenth century. Gilbert White once owned part of the estate: as a gentleman's residence Uppark is as superbly sited as any in England, high among woods on a hill that commands views across the Solent to the Isle of Wight.

Though 'downs' seems a misnomer to the cyclist, the long gradual descent, looping round park and pasture and woodland to West Marden, was effortless and exhilarating. The downs themselves seemed to swing round with the rider in a half-circle. The road continued skirting, climbing, dipping among the long smooth curves of pale brown soil or misty blue-green grassland to Walderton, Funtington, West and East Ashling in an ancient country of camps and barrows, tumuli and flintworks, as if in a world cut off from all connection with trunk roads and trailers. Then with a casual air it led me into Chichester.

Chichester has preserved the plan of its Roman origin

almost complete. The four main streets run north, south, east and west to meet at the beautiful, perpendicular fifteenth-century market cross (not improved by its eighteenth-century addition of a clock). Other streets also in the Pallant area keep their regular Roman lines. The outline of the walls, converted in part to banked-up public walks, is still preserved and near the deanery and cathedral more complete in form. The twelfth-century cathedral, although perhaps more provincial and homely than outstandingly handsome, dominates the scene and gives the town its 'air'—though not one of the decorous dullness sometimes considered ecclesiastical. Any first impression that otherwise Chichester is just a glorified market town is dispelled by looking more attentively along West Street, North Street and Little London. West Street has an incomparable Wren house, of red brick with pineapple gate piers —the pineapple having just come to England in Charles II's time. It may have been given its rough plans when Wren visited Chichester to repair the cathedral spire. Pallant House is a Georgian gem and carries a pair of ostriches on its gateposts. The Corn Exchange with its Doric columns also has elegance. Then there is a remarkable survival, a medieval hospital, St Mary's in St Martin's Square, where the fourteenth-century roof covers nave and two aisles partitioned off into rooms for the inmates. In complete contrast there is also the new Festival Theatre. Altogether, then, it is a town to look twice at, especially with sunshine in the close, the bustle of a colourful market and the sense of sea not far away, beyond South Street, and yachts' sails in Chichester Channel.

Three half-formed images, from discursive reading, chance recalled pictures, here combined to tempt me eastward again. They were of the historic splendour of ducal Arundel, its Windsor-like castle and steeply-pitched town, of the oriental fantasy of the Royal Pavilion, Brighton, backed by those unrivalled Regency terraces, and, midway between them, of the enormous Gothic chapel on the hill that stood for Lancing College, Victorian dream of a public school. They tantalised, but resistibly. I thought of the long, flat speedway from Chichester to Brighton and of the likelihood of a west wind down it, freshening off the sea, against my return. The sharpness of the images faded ...

So after a refresher I turned west, for another and even more striking site. Fishbourne, a few miles along the Portsmouth road, was opened to the public in 1968, after it had been lovingly excavated and restored by the Sussex Archaeological Trust. It is a Roman palace, the largest residence yet found in Britain and the only one built in true Italian style. Apparently the site was first a military base, created in AD 43, and survived as the residence of the local ruler 'rex et legatus Augusti in Britannia', Tiberius Claudius Cogidubnus, until its destruction by fire about AD 280. Quite the most attractive feature, to me, was the mosaic flooring of many of the rooms, unusually complete, and in the case of a winged-and-serpent-tailed seahorse, dramatically alive. The whole palace and Roman garden, with the excavated 'finds' on display, provided a fascinating gloss on times past in Chichester.

'Cycling, are you?' said a fellow loiterer. I'd stopped to lean over the sea wall and look at the yachts in Emsworth harbour.

'Not many do hereabout nowadays. But there's one fellow still going strong. Bought a Dursley-Pedersen, he did, just after they first came out and, summer days, he'll often be seen riding it about slowish like. Lives over Barnham way, does old Tom: it's only a small place, anyone will tell you where. He must be all of 93 now—puts his living so long down to his Dursley P.'

Seeing that the machine came on the market first as a gents' luxury model in the nineties and became well known about the turn of the century, I could believe the first statement about the rider's age. Other examples of the cantilever-built DPs continuing in use for anything up to fifty years also confirm the possibility of his persistence. He would have got the trim of the unique hammock saddle like second nature.

'Next time you're Barnham way you should look him up if he's still riding.'

I agreed and noted also that I must see Emsworth's other old tide mill next time. This late afternoon, after looking at the one on the jetty and at several attractive Georgian corners in this once prosperous little eighteenth-century port, I had to continue down the highway for Portsmouth.

But not for long. The sweep of traffic into the fast new coast road at Havant warned me to cut off for Portsdown Hill before being rushed through to Fareham and Southampton. Friendly hospitality awaited me, again, for that night, in the hinterland but within view of the hill's great Napoleonic forts . . .

From there, after morning admiration of the way a well-tended orchard and garden responds to Solent air, I made a short foray to Portsea Island and old Portsmouth. For traffic ease I took the road fork towards Southsea and just before crossing the railway turned right and into the under-belly of the town for the centre. A long, shabby street, herringboned with other, shorter, even shabbier streets and overflowing with old furniture, old clothes, old records and magazines, old crockery and old radio and every other sort of old crock shop—'slop shops' as Dickens would have called them—led straight to what once was, no doubt, an impressive urban heart. This has gone—bombing saw to that—apart from the rather grand Guildhall: what is left seems common to dockyard towns the world over, endless mean thoroughfares of exactly similar houses, plentifully interspersed with small pubs and gin-palaces, boarded-up clubs and dismal cafés, behind a few busy main streets with cinemas, a theatre, supermarket and Chinese restaurants. Portsmouth makes this contrast between mean and pretentious more striking by its new, hugely grotesque shopping precinct—the 'Tricorn'—a drab, grey ziggurat of half-occupied avenues of branch stores and stalls where watchmen with Alsatian dogs patrol to prevent damage or depredation. As a monument to civic aesthetic indifference it must be outstanding.

Pepys, who once lay at the Red Lion and walked round the town upon the walls, described Portsmouth as 'seeming to be a very pleasant and strong place.' Neither adjective, perhaps, would occur to the visitor today, until he penetrated past the tattooists', the corner pubs, the curry-and-chips or Bombay duck eating-places, and came to the great dockyard gates, the spick-and-span harbour hotels—one newly named after Sir Alec Rose's round-the-world sailing ship, the *Lively Lady*—the remains of the walls and the outlook over the vast naval anchorage. With the *Victory* in sparkling trim and, it may be, an aircraft carrier within a few cables' lengths, with the forts and Spithead and all the serried gantries and signal installations in view under the Downs, he might then change 'pleasant' to impressive, or under certain conditions of sun and wind and hardway activity, even to 'inspiring'.

Resisting the temptation to ferry across to Ryde on one of the new hovercraft, I returned to town centre and the main road to Hilsea. Here, at 387 Commercial Road, Landport— once Mile End Terrace—Charles Dickens was born and was christened at St Mary's, Portsea, his father being a navy pay-clerk. The house remains, a little less dingy than the rest, along with other reminders of a colourful past not bombed or cleared away such as the pub sign, the Air Balloon. From Hilsea I swung with the Southampton traffic, but only far enough to branch into Porchester, where the Romans built their guardian fort at the head of the harbour. Water still laps the Roman walls in one place, a Norman keep rises from within the earlier defences, but it is no longer the centre and protection of a town. The great shore stronghold, however, its massive masonry colonised by cheiranthus— indigenous form of the wallflower—and enclosing with its moat a wide green sward, is a pleasant retreat from the hurly-burly of the road. From the mud by the shore a flock of dunlin got up, wheeling and turning, and further off

Page 71 (above) Selborne Church, Hampshire; (below) the Camber Dock, Portsmouth, with the cathedral tower overlooking the scene

Page 72 (above) Winchester as seen from St Giles' hill, showing the Cathedral Church of St Swithin, consecrated in 1093; (below) A distant glimpse of Salisbury Cathedral from Harnham Mill, Wiltshire

brent geese were feeding, with no attention to spare for anyone or anything else.

So back, by the bright straggle of bungalows and cottages, genteel retirement houses and cafe-curio shops that compose modern Portchester to the A27 and from it, past the enclave of service houses and on to Portsdown again, with its crumbling brick forts of the sailing era and its modern admiralty establishment of the guided missile age, to reach my temporary home-from-home. Then, after supper, a final tremendous view from the darkened down of all that low-lying area: the myriad lights from buildings and streets and traffic and shopping intermingled in a mysterious panorama, comprising Hayling Island, Langstone Harbour, Portsea Island, Portsmouth Harbour, Gosport and Southampton Water, all meannesses and ugly modern modes obscured. At a glance it was not unlike the sprawling city of Bagdad as it appears by night to travellers on the old Damascus road. This, perhaps, is the best way of seeing the teeming complex of a future single Solent City.

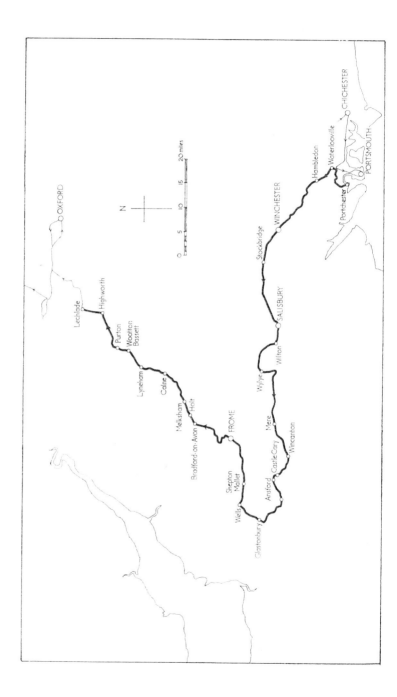

CHAPTER THREE

WESTWARD LOOK

Never act upon impulse when riding a bicycle, especially in the city. If you do you're sure to take someone by surprise and friction in the traffic near, if not accident, is sure to be the result.

'WHAT bicycle did you say this was of yours?' asked George. Harris told him. I forget what particular manufacture it happened to be: it is immaterial.

'Are you sure?' persisted George.

'Of course I am sure,' answered Harris. 'Why, what's the matter with it?'

'Well, it doesn't come up to the poster,' said George, 'that's all.'

'What poster?' asked Harris.

'The poster advertising this particular brand of cycle,' explained George. 'I was looking at one on a hoarding a day or two before we started. A man was riding this make of machine, a man with a banner in his hand: he wasn't doing any work, that was as clear as daylight; he was just sitting on the thing and drinking in the air. The cycle was going of its own accord, and going well. This thing of yours leaves all the work to me. It is a lazy brute of a machine; if you don't shove, it simply does nothing. I should complain about it if I were you.'

(Jerome K. Jerome: *Three Men on the Bummel*)

I had no complaint about 'Claud' so far, nor illusions— Life at no point realises the Poster—but I was glad to notice on the day after reaching Portsmouth that the westerly winds had dropped. There was practically a dead calm. Even though the sport of bicycling rarely consists of 'sitting on a luxurious saddle and being moved rapidly in the direction you wish to go by unseen heavenly powers' (as George's poster artist seemed to convey), it was possible now, and more pleasant, 'while sitting on the thing' to drink in the air without having to fight against it. I set off, without delay, towards Winchester and Salisbury.

Sun gave me a cheering start, as I crossed the A 3 to the minor road traversing the old Forest of Bere. Denmead, a signpost to World's End, then 'Cricket' Hambledon—where the game had its beginnings on Broad Halfpenny Down and the pub sign of the Bat and Ball shows a curved bat—and Droxford, where Izaak Walton once fished in the river Meon. Lambs dotted the down as white as daisies, beech glades were white-carpeted with wood anemones and in sheltered spots primroses covered the turf. The candelabra of a pale green whitebeam glittered against the sky. A string of ponies out at exercise came down the road, while the riding mistress stood near her mount broadside across it to shepherd them through a gate. The downs rolled ahead in continuous ridge and furrow, with scooped turfy hollows and open chalky downs fringed with scrub. It was tempting, this fine April morning, to follow one of the tracks, beyond the brown fields under the ridge, to whatever hamlet or vantage point they might lead.

From the brick-and-flint cottage and the fine bell tower of Droxford's church I swung again, away from the A 32, and into rolling down ways, verges sprinkled now with cowslips. *Right, right, right* urged the sign to Rycote House, but I kept straight on. The final ridge, after several that had deceptively promised to be the roof of the downs, gave a sensational panoramic view of Winchester, its great austere cathedral resplendent in the sun. To coast down the long, smooth curving descent into the city's maze of small streets felt not unlike 'moving by heavenly powers' in the direction one wished to go. Winchester, former capital of England, King Alfred's city, seat of a remarkable medieval school foundation, does not disappoint. I crossed the quadrangle of the school, founded by William of Wykeham in 1387, saw the fourteenth-century cloister and the 'old school' by Christopher Wren, the rows of neat Georgian houses and the great sprawl of nineteenth-century classrooms, eaves-dropped on an organ lesson in the chapel and looked out to the lonely clump of beeches on top of St Catherine's Hill. That such surroundings often have produced among pupils 'a sense of superiority, well-bred and impregnable to the envious attacks of inferiors' caused no surprise.

> *Make me, O sphere-descended Queen,*
> *A Bishop—or at least a Dean*

the Wykehamist used to pray to the goddess of learning. I stood in the Close before the immense grey length of Norman Bishop Walkelin's cathedral, one of the longest in Europe (526 feet) and, along with the inevitable Chinese sightseers walked among the tremendous aisles of England's heirlooms —among them being the tombs of King Alfred, of Izaak Walton and Jane Austen. It was more impressive, but only just, than Wykeham's school chapel which stands like a tall ship, moored to its graceful tower.

From the Plume of Feathers inn and the West Gate in the original defence wall—which the existence of the inn helped to preserve—to the elegant three-stage Cross, a fifteenth-century place of proclamation and punishment, and through the Broadway to the further end, the city's main thorough-fare holds both eye and imagination with its historic and architectural appeal. Its piazza on the south side, its paved courts and back lanes employ the patina of age to enhance modern fashion goods and bibelots display. All speaks of English, best southern English, taste, quality and tradition. Greenery and flowers, Bath stone and sunlight add their gaiety . . . Striding aloofly along, with a tan that spoke of hotter suns than those of an English spring and with eyes fixed apparently on some personal vista of Himalayan peaks, turning his back on the everyday world, a master threaded his way through the strollers on his way back to school like an eagle to its eyrie.

Winchester has more than its share of fine old buildings, but one, the medieval Hospital of St Cross, to which I asked the way of a young constable, eluded him. Founded originally 'for the subsistence of thirteen resident poor men in every necessity of life' by Bishop Henry de Blois, brother of King Stephen, and providing a hundred other poor people with a dinner daily, it was enlarged by William of Wykeham —and it still offers to the traveller a modest *viaticum* from the chantry. When I mentioned that one could get a dole of ale and bread there, 'Oh, you mean the "spike"' said the constable. 'No, there's none here. Newbury's the nearest. That's where I send travellers [ie tramps] when they've had a night at Portsmouth "spike" [workhouse].' St Cross and the way-farer's 'loaf of five measures and drink in sufficient quantity' being actually a mile out of my way, to the south of Winchester, I settled instead for my regular 'dole', shandy and sandwich, in a pub near the Close. Shandy here cost 9p instead of 6p—a 50 per cent levy for the upkeep of the premises?

The road out to Stockbridge was all pitch and roll, the downs presenting their corrugations, in folds from north to south as well as from east to west. If it was not quite as arduous as the constable imagined—still enervated, perhaps, by his recent 'Outward Bound' training course in the central Lake District—I was glad that no westerly wind blew. Stockbridge, well known for its fishing on the Test, is little more than a street of antiques-cum-pubs-cum-snackbars. It is a glaring example of the fate that overtakes presentable villages on west-country motoring routes. A mile or two further on, at a National Trust downland viewpoint, Danebury Hill, there was a picnic-cum-parking place. It and all the surrounding bins overflowed with can, bottle and carton rubbish. A 'canalised' nuisance, perhaps one says, and better than spreading it over the whole countryside: but why not make a clearance first and then start enforcing the penalties?

I crossed a tributary of the Test, which comes down by the Wallops, Over, Middle and Nether, so far an unpolluted valley of lush water-meadows, purling stream, black-and white cattle, then at Lobscombe corner came to where the main roads from Newbury and Basingstoke join to feed westbound traffic down to Yeovil, Honiton and Exeter. Cars whizzed by at fifty-, forty-, thirty-yard intervals. The extensive, if somewhat monotonous views of shallow bowls of downland tillage and bosky slopes were to be enjoyed only at imminent risk. After a sufficient dose of this I sought the mild restorative of tea at a pull-in café.

The menu offered:

EXECUTIVES BREAKFAST:
Fruit juice.
Double egg, hashed brown potatoes,
Black pudding,
Tomato, bacon.

Then, as if thinking better of it:

LUNCH – INCREASE THE SPACE BEHIND THE WHEEL:
Unsweetened fruit juice.
Salmon salad platter,
Brown rye bread.
Fruit yoghurt.

There were also:

MEALS FOR MY SMALL FRIENDS:
Crisply Fried Fish Fingers
French Frys [sic]
(A small CHOC BAR FREE for every clean plate.)

Other large cafeterias punctuated the final miles into Salisbury, disgorging cars haphazard into the traffic. The road edges added their peril of corrugated surface on the long swinging descent. But the spire in the middle foreground claimed at least half my attention. Not only the highest, but one of the loveliest in England, it is also the immediate focus of the city from wherever one sees it. The city itself has been called 'the apple of the eye of England'.

It took some little time here to find accommodation. I drew blank at two private hotels, a pub, two transport and tourist houses, a students' lodging and a superior guest-house. Finally I 'homed' on a neat 'semi', with box-hedging and espaliered apple trees, which formerly had been on the CTC list. (Although as a member I carried the handbook of addresses, I seldom went out of my way to track them down, preferring to go by the feel of the place and traveller's intuition.) The 'semi' was comfortable, modest in price for bed and breakfast—and excessively genteel. Helen Hamilton, Ontario, was another guest. I read her name in the book, heard her voice, but my landlady's management of meal times, use of bathroom, breakfast room and billpaying prevented my curiosity about a middle-aged Canadian's presence being satisfied, by as much as a glimpse. Even my bicycle was removed from sight, where it stood under the eaves outside the breakfast room, in order to ensure Miss (Mrs?) Hamilton's privacy. I was curious, for one thing, about the reason why she was not staying at one of the superior guest-houses, which set out to cater for American, German and other continental tourists. A cut above the boarding-house and slightly below hotel class, they fix their charges midway between and make much play of their central heating, *full* breakfast and their *linen* (not nylon) sheets.

It was Sunday: a hundred-strong Salvation Army band was in procession to Salisbury's market square as I went out in search of an evening meal. Gathered in the capacious square and baroomphing away on its trombones and tubas the band seemed to emphasise the fact that new Sarum, apart from the cathedral, is in essence a large country town in agricultural surroundings. It has not grown higgledy-piggledy through Roman, Saxon and Norman times, as have most similar cities, but was mapped out with the site of the cathedral, unhampered and in entirely new ground, early in the thirteenth century following conflict between castle and cathedral interests in cramped Old Sarum. As the cathedral has benefited in architectural uniformity of style and in the spacious close that surrounds its double cross plan, so the open, airy streets on a more regular plan than is usual benefit the citizen. Overlying this today there is a cultural atmosphere about the quiet streets and houses off-centre reminiscent of Cambridge.

After ravioli and a glass of Beaujolais in the only eating-place open, I sampled the sights. Such buildings as the thirteenth-century deanery and Mompesson House, formelry Judges' lodging, in the close, or in the approach to it the Collegium Matronarum MDCLXXXI, keep the eye down, in case some other architectural treasure should be missed, as much as the 404-foot cathedral spire would elevate it. The embattled precinct gates, which punctuate the rampart wall built round the Close in times of conflict, rival Winchester's gates in interest. St Ann's Gate, not far from my lodging, led into a quiet narrow street in which every house and antique shop showed character. Various buildings in the town still betray their former use of origin—STEAM PRINTING WORKS is written high and large over a modern facade—but regrettably Poultry Cross, circa 1300, next to the fourteenth-century Haunch of Venison inn, is almost enclosed by shops. In addition to such obvious features as the King's Arms, refuge of Charles II, and the fine timbered Old George inn not far from St Thomas Church in the High Street, the dignity and spaciousness of the quieter streets behind the market-place are in themselves rewarding. The town, of course, has its tourist bait and its trend away from earlier craft guild and market interests. 'There's only one fish shop in the place,' grumbled my landlady, as I was leaving next morning, 'it's all carpets and TV sales nowadays.' More ominously, the Department of the Environment now agrees to the construction of an elevated road and car park in this 'apple of the eye of England.'

Salisbury is situated at the confluence of the rivers Avon,

Bourne and Wylye. I set out by Wilton—famous for Wilton House and its Inigo Jones double-cube room and, equally to some, for the unrivalled Palladian bridge over the Nadder —in order to enjoy the morning delights of the gentle Wylye. Drooping willows, primroses, the flash of a yellow-bellied stoat: footbridges across clear purling streams: cottages of knapped flint and limestone squares in chequer-board pattern: pastoral quiet lapping the water-meadows around Steeple Langford, Hanging Langford and Wylye village. To keep away from the frenzy of the A 30 as long as possible I turned up out of the vale and over the down to Dinton. From the ridge a narrow way dropped down between flinty banks into the village as into a well: I kept height, skimming along the edge towards Telfont Magna, with wide views over vale and woodland. Then to Chilmark where Ye Olde Black Dog promised well and lived up to its promise with a satisfying 'ploughman's lunch'. A mini cottage loaf, two slabs of cheese, two onions, tomato, cucumber, lettuce and two portions of butter, with shandy, for 18½p.

'You do like sitting in pubs, don't you?'

'Well . . . it depends on the pub, terribly . . .'

Some of the regulars, like the Black Dog, were inclined to the chi-chi, but with all its three-legged stools and mock-antique lanterns, its row of pewter measures and green floral upholstery, its inglenook with radiant heat and steady gin-drinkers, it was fair and friendly to the passing cyclist.

After Fonthill Bishop and Hindon I came on to the A 303 and a monotone of down-end country, where huge areas of stony, fenceless ploughland were bisected by a switchback route of long, slow ascents and fast, twisting descents. The lay-by's were choked with rubbish: heavy traffic and its fumes assaulted the sense. A village such as Mere—one of those old stone villages, all Georgian inns and trim houses, that become antiquities living on antiques, was slowly being murdered by it. Who could imagine now the Dorset poet William Barnes holding school in its Tudor chantry? Peace, security, even fabric were being relentlessly destroyed. I laboured on to Zeals, past the sign to Stanton and the great house and classically ornamented gardens of Stourhead, under a sky that was becoming overcast with a misty hint of drizzle. Then across the river Stour and by the appropriately named Stoke Trister into Wincanton. The small, steeply pitched market town was no place to halt: its traffic saw to that. I turned away with relief from the London–Exeter maelstrom and away from the threat of Shaftesburian rain—the kind that lasts for twenty-four hours—away from the Dorset–Somerset border country towards Castle Cary.

Almost immediately sun broke through, fields turned a richer green, hill-top farms invited the eye up narcissus-bordered lanes, and in hazel copses bird song was audible again. With the dumpling of Creech Hill as landmark I climbed steadily through estate lands to the top of Cary Hill, from which on a good day one can see shipping in the Bristol Channel. An old lodge-keeper—relic of the great days of a mansion that was now three-quarters empty—told me to go to the Waggon and Horses, if I wanted friendly service.

I did, but the Lancashire-born landlord regretted his accommodation was full. He was genuinely sorry to refuse: his own relatives were always visiting 'now we've come south' and he could not keep even one room vacant. Instead he directed me to a bungalow up the lane, 'but come back here if you can't get in'. There again it turned out that an aunt was occupying the only spare room. The owner, however, kindly telephoned two of her friends and came back to say that I would be welcome at 'Nippy's Rest', another bungalow at the Ansford end of the town. I found it easily enough, and within fifteen minutes, although the accommodation was offered only as bed and breakfast, I was sitting down to half the family's evening meal, roast pork, sprouts, baked potatoes, apple sauce, fruit and fresh cream, in spite of my initial protests. While her husband had the other half my good landlady made for herself a scratch supper, after protests and apologies, in turn, that she had not been ready for guests. Rare hospitality.

Afterwards in the mild, flower-scented dusk I called again at the Waggon and Horses to thank the landlord for, indirectly, leading me to 'Nippy's Rest'. He had first come down to these parts, he said, about fifteen years previously, with a cycling club from Stockport. Knowing northern clubs by repute I breathed in—and out, again, as he added that they only did about fifty miles a day. They always used Youth Hostels, then packed with cyclists. Where are they now, he asked? He had bought his son a bike, a good one at over £30, and he had been out on it about twice. No one seemed to cycle for pleasure any longer. What on earth had come over them? I dropped a hint about the A 303 and other doomways of 'tinman in his motorcan', to save the lad from excess of parental displeasure. As I was leaving him to his locals he called: 'How do you like it at "Nippy's Rest"? *There's* a live wire for you. Do you know why he calls his house that? It's because rest is what he never could, and Nippy's his nickname.'

∗   ∗   ∗

From Nippy's garden the following morning—after he had left the house to drive his early workmen's bus—I could see as far as Hinckley Point, or at any rate the nuclear power station there, on the Bristol Channel. It was an admirable day. The curve of Castle Cary's single long street encouraged loitering. Its hand-railed causeway, its colonnaded market hall, its octagonal 'lock-up' and its church set on the hill made photographic interest and for once the sun was right. A fortunate little market-town, sequestered on its byroad, sheltered and little spoiled by development. Its inhabitants and those of Mere were at opposite poles for the enjoyment of living. Not surprising that it is a land of cosy retirement bungalows and eking-out B & B.

Still in warming sun, I took now the village way that 'Nippy' had recommended, by Alford, East Lydford, over the Fosse Way and along the Somerton Road to Kineton

Mandeville. Alford's mineral spring once attracted visitors
there to take the cure, but as there was no good accommodation for people of fashion—according to Celia Fiennes,
indefatigable sampler of spas at the turn of the seventeenth
century—many people sent for the waters and had them
brewed into beer instead. The waters were 'mostly from
Alum, a cleare little well and a quick spring—a quick purge
good for all sharp humors or obstructions' (*Journeys: 1685–
1703*). Other attractions to the area were then, no doubt, as
now, the cowslip meadows, the orchards with lambs frolick-
ing under appleblossom, the slow-moving willow-bordered
'rhines' criss-crossing the rich pasture and, shortly, the
distant, blue-misted view of Glastonbury's conical Tor. Here
I relished country quiet and the feeling of a way of life,
leisurely, agricultural, self-sufficient, based on a confident
pride in the Somerset heritage and on enjoyment of its
varied scene, plain, coast, hill and gorge. Almost without
noticing the wheels turning in these gentle lanes, I came by
Barton St David, Butleigh, Butleigh Wootton and out of
dream on to the level road across the vale to the legendary
Arthurian Isle of Avalon (Welsh=Isle of Apples) and
Glastonbury.

Not busy at this time of year, the town was friendly and
hospitable. Only the owner of an antique shop with a NO
HIPPIES sign gave me a boiled lobster glare as I passed
through his ground floor premises to an upstairs bookshop
in search of a map. There were several features of special
interest: the Pilgrim's Inn (now the George) in High Street,
where fifteenth-century travellers found their accommodation when there was no room at the Abbey; and the
Tribunal, near to it, once court-house for cases over which
the Abbot held jurisdiction. The slender Gothic market
cross is modern: even more so the trendy boutique Pat Li
Shun, formed of a couple of cottages painted with large
bright sunflowers round door and windows, like medieval
saints' aureoles.

The real cynosures, of course, are Glastonbury Tor—

recognised by St Joseph of Arimathea, who had been sent
to preach the gospel, as 'most like to Tabor's holy mount';
Glastonbury thorn, said to have sprouted from the saint's
staff planted at the point where he landed on Wearyall Hill;
and Glastonbury Abbey. The Norman porch of this and St
Joseph's chapel are the least fragmentary remains—the
Abbey became a stone quarry for the neighbourhood after
the Dissolution—but the appeal is as much mystical as
architectural. Here, according to tradition, have been the
sepulchres of King Arthur and his Queen Guinevere, of
Kings Edmund, Edgar and Edmund Ironside, of St Dunstan
and of St Joseph of Arimathea himself.

The most direct route to Wells is over East Sedgemoor
along a causeway constructed from masonry torn from the
Abbey walls. I followed the modern version and half-way
came to The Blue Bowl, an old cider house. The sign
showed a punch bowl, with lemon and ladle and blue glass
bottle—Bristol 'blue'?—and the beer handles were of
willow-pattern china. The house-cum-smallholding was not
less than two hundred years old. Once every farm labourer
had used it as his cider-house, but times change even Somerset habits. No cider served now—the old 'scrumpy' was too
powerful. No mild either—only two or three pubs served it
between there and Bristol: and no cheese. So shandy it was
again, and a glazed, plastic-embalmed pie.

Polsham, Coxley and then, as the views back to the Polden
Hills diminished, the rise of the Mendips ahead and the
bijou city of Wells. Though it is little different from
Glastonbury in size of population, dignity and spaciousness
are added to its market-place area by the central setting of
the cathedral and bishop's palace, with their surrounding
green and moat. The streets were still in their post-lunch
torpor and as yet without trippers so that I could savour
fourteenth-century houses and obscure little yards, Vicars
Close, a delightful double row with picturesque gables and
high chimneys, ancient gateways—Penniless Porch, Dean's
Eye and Palace Eye—without distraction. By the moat, of

course, and at the drawbridge where 'educated swans' ring a bell for food, a Chinese student was standing rapt. If she had also seen Lincoln, Winchester and Salisbury, as I had, she would perhaps have agreed that the palm should be given for sheer beauty to Wells's west front. A 'hymn of stone', with tier upon tier of matchless statuary, and of majestic but graceful proportions, it ranks as the finest existing example of Early English architecture. The peaceful cloistered atmosphere that seemed to spread from it like ripples in a quiet pool, over green lawns and gardens and time-worn stone, into the surrounding city was nothing short of Trollopian.

The road leading out to Shepton Mallet offers one of the finest views of the cathedral, as an architectural group in all its harmony and variety. With that as valediction I turned away from Avalon and Camelot, Athelney and Wedmore, this land of Arthur and Alfred (the bishopric of Wells was founded, 909, by Edward the Elder, son of Alfred the Great) and towards mundane bed and breakfast. An uneventful few miles by Croscombe—whose church is as distinguished for the carving of its pulpit, screen and pews as it seems to be unvisited—brought me to a very different place, Shepton Mallet itself.

The town had a run-down dispirited air, almost as lost-looking as some old mining town at its lower end, where empty and half-empty shops, second-hand clothes and fourth-hand furniture stores, a straggle of pet shops and junk displays—'You only stock what you know you can sell' said one owner of frowsty rubbish—jostle together near the railway line to Radstock. It all spreads from a hill-top crossroads (Yeovil–Bristol) down past the market-place and into the valley where a service road to a new estate undercuts the main-road bridge as in some Lowry painting. Formerly three times its present size, Shepton was the refuge of Huguenot weavers, whose dilapidated cottages line the valley bottom. They are gradually to be restored and could make this area picturesque, even pleasant, despite the Babycham factory facing them. A fifteenth-century market cross on the Salisbury pattern, old shambles and an impressive church with hammer-beam roof are other features capable of lending interest in an unduly neglected part of the town.

The Shrubbery Hotel, AA, RAC etc, was changing hands the following week and not inclined to bother with a 'single' —always at a disadvantage in overnight accommodation— let alone a cyclist. It had been recommended as 'the only place in Shepton for you' by a passing cleric, who also sometimes did bed and breakfast, but his vicarage was six miles out of my way. When I said I'd take dinner, however, the 'Shrubbery' consented to find me a perch. Its restaurant, open to non-residents, was a tastefully decorated cellar: the diners, with me and a solitary commercial, totalled four: the dinners, also tasteful, were prepared by a sixteen-year-old girl 'chef'. There were wines—white, red, rose—for those wishing to 'celebrate' in Shepton Mallet.

Hotel ownership has its own perils, apart from uncertainties of custom. The Shrubbery's owner, I learnt, having built and fitted with his own built-in furniture a bungalow for retirement in the hotel grounds, had sold out to a manager of some licensed premises who was anxious to relinquish the ties of pub hours. He was the tenant of the brewery and any bedroom lets were his 'perks'. Recently a disastrous hotel fire elsewhere had been followed by a new law requiring the provision of outside escapes to all hotel bedrooms. The brewery, he soon found, disclaimed all responsibility. So he, the vacating tenant, had to find the cost, estimated at £3,000, of fixing escapes before he could pass on the letting goodwill.

*   *   *

Leaving the commercial at breakfast with the paper he had ordered 'because I like to read the strips', I was off next morning on the road to Frome, while most of Shepton still slept. A cool north-west breeze, hazy sun and a sense of

Page 89 (above) The village of Mere, Wiltshire; (below) Glastonbury Tor, Somerset

Page 90 (above) Bradford-on-Avon, Wiltshire, with its fifteenth-century bridge spanning the river. The chapel on the bridge has served as a lock-up and a toll-house; *(below)* St John's Lock, near Lechlade—the first lock on the river Thames

escape from depression put a little extra into my wheels up the hill to Doulting and on down the A 361 to Holwell. There I struck what was probably the worst stretch of the whole tour—to call it 'murder mile' would be no exaggeration. At this end of the Mendips are situated the English China Clay quarries, the biggest of their kind in Europe. From the works exit the road in the direction of Frome mounts on blind bends and between high banks. When, as happened nearly continuously, long vehicles and trucks in convoy passed each other in this confined space there was no extra clearance at all—and no means of escape off the road. They seldom reduced speed and so I was reduced to walking up the hill, on the down traffic side, ready to fling myself into the hedge. Fortunately this did not last long. The road levelled out again: by the time I had realised which by-road it was that afforded a glimpse of Longleat House, Macaulay's 'most magnificent country house in England', graced by the view from 'Heaven's Gate' and seat of the Marquess of Bath, I was well past it and already in the outskirts of Frome.

This prosperous little market town (pronounced 'Froom') provided compensations. A woollen, printing and brewing centre, it is picturesquely built on a hillside and keeps several streets entirely free of traffic. As I was walking along the raised causeway of one towards Catherine Hill, a veteran CTC member stopped beside me. 'Claud' had aroused interest again. He admired the lug work, felt the tyre pressure and after expert scrutiny pointed out that the rear wheel ran slightly off true. As we righted it he told me that he was now sixty-six and had just realised a life-long ambition—cycling more than a thousand miles to visit the Rhineland and his father's relatives there. His former favourite cycling playground had been the Dukeries, but with traffic as it was today . . . He wished me the best of luck.

A little further on, at 'cheese wedge' corner, where one narrow eighteenth-century house-end separates two streets, a young coin dealer invited me to take coffee in his shop, out of interest in the 'tour' and readiness to talk about his trade. He had taken it up not very long before, when he gave up the 'rat race'—in this case maintenance engineering —and decided to do instead what he really enjoyed. Putting expensive machines to rights every day for workmen who could not or would not use them without wrecking them again seemed to him a poor game compared with handling fine gold and silver or acquiring first-hand knowledge of porcelain and glass. He was not the only public-school product I was to meet who felt likewise about his pre-ordained career.

After that introduction to Frome ways I walked downhill to the bright and busy open market, and to neighbouring Cheap Street. No traffic here, but a 'kennel' or water runnel after the fashion of the Persian 'jube' down the middle of the street and arched over it symbolic shop signs, such as a large, gilded loaf of bread. Framed by the gables at the end there rose the Perpendicular spire of St John's church, whose exterior carries a notable Via Crucis—a series of carvings representing the Steps to Calvary. With the river Avon at its foot and the tiered rise of irregular, narrow stone streets such as Stony Street and Palmer Street, Frome was a pleasant discovery.

Still anxious to be rid of traffic's roar and fume, I took wandering by-roads to Bradford-on-Avon. In estate-country quiet, among fat lambs and shining furrows, cowslip fields and tall hedgerows I meandered to Beckington, Laverton, Woolverton and Rode. At Rode, a Bass Charrington head-quarters, the Cross Keys could offer only a stereotyped meat pie and shandy, but there was a most singular church to make up. It stood high and at the west entry it had two large pinnacles, like Indian *stupas,* instead of the usual spire or tower. The verger suggested that the building of the church had been 'gentry's whim' on return from their travels.

From Rode to Farleigh and Bradford-on-Avon I faced north by west and so into the wind. The last few miles of my first five hundred were as hard going as those at the beginning. Rain threatened, but sun was just off-stage and as I reached that splendid museum-town of silvery grey stone it gave the full *lumière* treatment. The immaculate Georgian mills, the Tudor Hall, the unaltered Saxon church, the rows of weavers' houses, the curious chapel on the bridge, all the courts and high-walled alleys were illuminated with a sudden brilliance, making a harmonious composition that could out-Bath Bath. A solitary canoeist shot the nine-arched bridge, willows and dignified mills mingled their reflections in the water, a couple of retired Australians loitered to look by the 'Old Forge' (tea-rooms) but apart from this muted activity Bradford—so different from that other whose postmark declares it MEANS BUSINESS—remained in its timeless trance. It was half-day closing. Not even one of the galaxy of antique shops showed signs of life. I saw a uniquely beautiful stone town as though frozen in its own perfection.

Pursued again by heavy trucks and container lorries through Holt, I continued to Melksham, still in sun, and across the eighteenth-century river bridge into a town that was, in 'cure' days, a would-be spa. It was so pounded by traffic that I felt no inclination to look for its converted Pump Room or to sample its quality further. So over by Melksham Forest, where wide views opened, to the southeast, of the bare escarpment of Warminster Down and Tenantry Down, and clear chalk tracks ran over to the army training area of Salisbury Plain. Cowslips and early bluebells, a brown, sluggish grass snake sunning itself in the dead leaves on the forest fringe: in the open stud stables and cloche-cultivated market gardens, the smell of pig manure and fertiliser punctuated my ride through a kind of no-man's land to Calne.

'Counting the suicides and the homicides?' I interrupted the constable who breasted the evening rush of traffic down Calne hill.

'Ah, we can but try: it gets worse every week,' he responded. I asked him about a bed-and-breakfast place.

'There's only one place here for such as yourself—a guesthouse just beyond the Cross. If that's full the next is at

Chippenham. We don't get many asking for it here. Wilt-shire,' he added, 'has nothing for the tourist except Stone-henge.'

The guest-house was not full, but neither was it open. I disregarded the constable's next suggestion and found a welcome instead in Kerry Crescent, at a transport drivers' boarding-house. If cleanliness, cheapness, friendliness, end-less supplies of hot water and large, punctual meals were the criterion, this was as good as any of my overnight halts. I was just in time for the three-course dinner at 6.15 pm—breakfast was 'on' from 6.15 am.

Calne, best known for one commodity, sausage, was to many men in wartime the town nearest to camp. Numbers of RAF personnel returned there afterwards, often to marry local girls, and the town's size increased two or threefold. By the long arm of coincidence I shared a table at Kerry Crescent with a civilian 'works and bricks' overseer of RAF building, who was just due to retire after wartime service and then a further twenty-five years' post-war service at my own RAF training base, Yatesbury. 'Which block were you in?' he asked, 'I saw the building of 'em all.' But after nearly thirty years I could not remember . . . There was an atmosphere about Calne's 'night-town'—aircraft with their green and red navigation lights overhead, dark blue sky with a full moon rising above the church tower, the narrow, shadowy street of pubs behind Harris's sausage factory with its warm, succulent breath, the Builder's Arms, where every new customer was welcomed on entering with a joke and a drink and where the darts league in session, experts all, had wide moustaches and premature pot-bellies. There was even a smack still of wartime and its exigencies, when the young 'truckie' wanted to book in his girl from Bristol for the night. The landlady at Kerry Crescent had no room vacant, but she offered the couchette and clean sheets in the TV lounge, clearing us out with cheerful camaraderie at 11 pm and giving the 'truckie' a wink and the key. It had been done before.

The Wiltshire uplands certainly had their share of army camp and aircraft runway bleakness. Absence of hedges, the cold, now north-east wind blowing across the wide fields, the vast concrete sheds, the regimented married quarters and, between-times, the large poultry farms and other animal barracks, made the day feel even more grey than it was. Road edges were full of holes and bumps, even though the grass verges were wide and correctly cut, distracting my eyes from the extensive view to Hackpen Hill, the Marlborough Downs and, after Wootton Bassett, into the Vale of White Horse. The railway museum at Wootton, the stocks and the ornamental black-and-white town hall gave interest to an essentially one-street town, but I had my sights fixed elsewhere on this uncompromising morning. At Purton I left the Cricklade road for by-lanes. Still spring-like in their blackthorn and cherry blossom, their violets and cowslips, but not in warmth, they led towards Blunsdon St Andrew, the Fosse Way—which cuts diagonally through Wiltshire like an imperial, not merely national highway— and over it to Broad Blunsdon and Highworth. One other hint of the season relieved the intervening landscape. A car was pulled up on the broad grass verge, its seats tilted back, and as I passed, its red-faced occupant half rose from his face-down position—obviously having a man's way with a maid.

Highworth has been called by our present poet laureate one of the most charming and unassuming country towns in the West of England. It also happens to be in Wiltshire but is not much praised in guide books, which may serve to excuse my Calne constable's oversight. Before its charm could work I called, first, at The Fishes and over sandwiches met my first fellow touring cyclists. They were husband and wife snatching a couple of days off on their Carlton 'Corsas' and fully intending that their young children should join them in cycling as soon as old enough. The Wantage area and the Vale of White Horse, they said, saw few pairs of wheels on the roads in summer. They themselves had toured the Cotswolds and Sussex and were hoping next year to tackle the Yorkshire dales. Oxford, from which they had come, had three cycling clubs, including the one attached to the University, and even supported its own cycling magazine, the *Oxford Cyclist*. Cheering news from a place of enlightenment.

A couple of farm girls came into the bar, one with a paper bag of chips and a cold, barefoot infant, who was promptly sick on the floor.

'Isn't she cold?' the cyclist's wife asked hesitantly.

'No: depends how you bring 'em up. All my children go barefoot: get used to it,' replied the mother. 'Do you want some music on?' She inserted a coin in the juke box, to drown the child's howling, while the publican fetched a cloth . . . Time to move.

The High Street of Highworth has arched ways leading to narrow lanes between garden walls, or into cobbled yards where coaches once drew in. Its virtues, like its church, are somewhat retiring. The tower is visible almost everywhere: but the church porch and lime-shaded churchyard can be glimpsed only through one of the archways. Apart from old bay-windowed inns and a fine, large red-brick Georgian house, the other attractions lie off the main thoroughfare, in and around the market-place, Sheep Street and Vicars Lane. The mixture of pale Cotswold stone and old brick, of painted white wooden porches, uneven stone-tiled or slate roofs, tall stone or brick chimney stacks, with wistaria or even vines trained against house fronts, is heady and nostalgic. Without all the hurrying Swindon traffic and without the overhead wires zig-zagging across it, the High Street too might attract more attention to this unexpected charmer set on its commanding hill above the Vale. As with Thame, its manner is peculiarly English.

The few miles on to Lechlade bridged the last stretch of borderland between the West Country and the Midlands— on a road unfortunately widened and straightened to take container lorries and the like. A brief diversion at Inglesham, to see the little church down by the Thames, whose clear glass, box pews, old screen and wall paintings William Morris saved from 'restoration', and then I was crossing Halfpenny Bridge and passing the toll cottage into this first Gloucestershire village. (Lechlade can scarcely be called 'town' for all its hotels, steak-bar, tea-rooms, beer-gardens, boat traffic and its five or six antique shops.) As I was looking at one of the displays admiring a large, old, gilded alabaster figure of Gautama Buddha and speculating from which despoiled temple it had come, a voice at my elbow said: 'Looking for rooms?'

The owner of it introduced himself as Mr Menzies and as the one-time keen rider of a 'Freddie Grubb', then much later of a Moulton small-wheel, which he had soon discarded —'like riding through a field of treacle', as he put it. He had also had a machine fitted with special Bill Bailey forks (until recently the Grand Old Man of British cycling) but had found this nowhere near as good up the hills nor as 'lively' as either the Grubb or Butler bicycle. It was a long time since he had seen a Claud B on the road. Was I staying here overnight or going on into the Cotswolds? If it was not too early for me to call a halt he could recommend a cottage in Lechlade, a once favoured CTC calling-place. It still had its large winged sign up. Or, if this was full, he added, with the fellowship of a cyclist, I must come to his own place.

Early as it was, I thought I would try the CTC cottage, and, if it offered a room, rest 'Claud' a while and walk for a change. 'Holmelea' welcomed me—'used to get a lot of your sort, but not nowadays in this traffic'—and I set out to enjoy the neighbourhood.

The crowded boatyard at Halfpenny Bridge showed what the summers brought to Lechlade. But to walk now along the Thames tow-path was to enjoy a pastoral scene such as William Morris must have known when he lived at nearby Kelmscot Manor. Only swans and ducks were mirrored in the oil-less water, willows framed the delicacy of the slender spire, late sun glowed from the creamy walls of the big house. A moorhen and flotilla of chicks emerged from a reedy backwater to enjoy its warmth before the river turned silver under evening's dove-grey sky. I sought the church and Shelley's Walk, among the great cedars, where apropos a summer evening in the churchyard, 1815, he wrote:

> *Here could I hope that death did hide*
> *From human sight sweet secrets.*

I tried the by-lanes that plunged straight into deep country towards the Leach and tempted one to follow that river through to East Leach and North Leach on the Fosse Way near to its source. Then I traversed again the trim streets of Lechlade, where such ornaments as an old sundial or a blue sun fire insurance sign or even a pair of antlers come naturally on cottage walls—this time in search of a meal.

The 'Lime Tree' café was almost closing, but before he went home the dedicated Welsh proprietor—'soup's done, I'm afraid: I always make it myself'—saw that I had a generous tomato omelette, crusty bread, luncheon's remains of orange sponge pudding and a welcome large pot of tea. It had to last me until morning.

So to 'Holmelea', with its pink mats and pink rugs and pink carpet, its bright blue flower-and-bird wallpaper, its pink-and-cream or pale green-and-cream door panels, its porcelain door plates decorated with roses and THIS IS IT for the lavatory, a butler-and-salver for the guest room, a chef-and-sirloin for the dining room, and with almost as many unexpected steps between bed and board as there were knick-knacks on every conceivable shelf or ledge. The presence of two large TV sets and three massive contract workers glued for the evening to them sent me early to rest, in a room overlooking Shelley's moonlit cedars.

CHAPTER FOUR

MIDLAND LINK

The life of a pneumatic tyre may be prolonged indefinitely
if one picks out the small flints that may have lodged in the
outer cover, and fills up the cuts with morsels of cotton wool
soaked.

My obvious course from Lechlade was to Burford, but on a whim I went first to Oxford for a night. What is so satisfying about travelling, about making journeys, as someone said recently, is that you are forced to leave all regimentation behind. The element of chance is very strong. 'You must be open to accident'. No doubt the remark applied to journeys in remoter places than England, but I shared the feeling and the tendency.

Oxford reintroduced itself via Eynsham and Hinksey, with first a smart riverside pub/restaurant, then a country house Buddhist retreat, then pairs of spectacled students out walking by the cowslip fields, then snug villas and the charisma of college towers and church spires ahead.

> *In the two Hinkseys nothing keeps the same;*
> *The village street its haunted mansion lacks,*
> *And from the sign is gone Sibylla's name,*
> *And from the roofs the twisted chimney-stacks.*
> (Arnold: 'Thyrsis')

Whatever changes the poet lamented there, Oxford seemed to call for no lament unless that 'plus ça change, plus c'est la meme pose'. There were robed and shaven young Buddhist

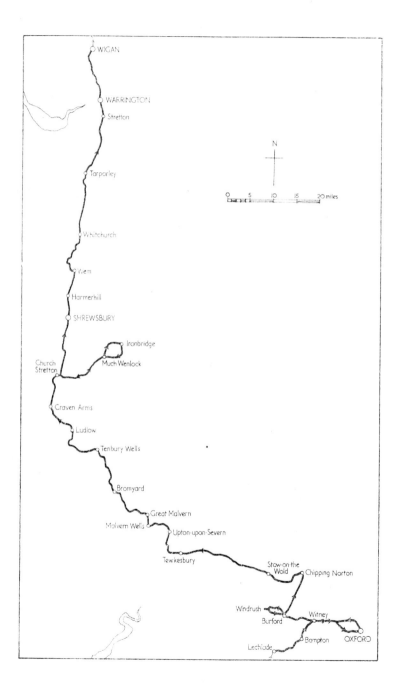

WIGAN

WARRINGTON

Stretton

Tarporley

Whitchurch

Wem

Harmerhill

SHREWSBURY

Ironbridge

Much Wenlock

Church
Stretton

Craven Arms

Ludlow

Tenbury Wells

Bromyard

Great Malvern

Malvern Wells

Upton-upon-Severn

Tewkesbury

Stow-on-the
Wold

Chipping Norton

Windrush

Witney

Burford

Lechlade

Bampton

OXFORD

N

0   5   10   15   20 miles

followers parading, drumming and chanting in the High:
there were bearded, shaggy-haired drop-outs sitting about in
poshtins on doorsteps in St John's Street: there were 'chic'
girls whose wardrobe seemed to be the chance relics of a
Victorian charity bazaar. But there were also St John's college gardens with their choice tulips and camellias at prime,
as immemorial as was the vista of St Giles in mellow sun,
or the select bootmakers and booksellers in the Turl, or that
familiar glimpse of St Mary's church with the Radcliffe
Camera and the Bodleian in view or the chimes of Great Tom.
Oxford has moods which change every five years or so as its
inhabitants change, but underneath Oxford has a warmer,
more domesticated atmosphere than its rival—and that
in spite of the fact that everyone who does not possess a
bicycle possesses a motor-bike or motor-car, so that it is rarely
possible to cross the road except at a hunted run. Few towns
in England leave upon the mind such an impression of congestion, subordinated to charm.

'*Everything* keeps the same' could be said about the lodg-
ing-houses, as far as my experience went. I found a ground-
floor 'gentleman's' room in St John Street, bed and breakfast
for a modest £1.60, after a little parleying about the bicycle
and my assurance that a 'drop-out' who had sidled up was not
in tow. NO BATH WITHOUT PREVIOUS ARRANGEMENT greeted
my entry: NO WASHING CLOTHES: then, ELECTRIC FIRE ON
METRE (sic). When breakfast came next morning—all meals
served in rooms on a tray—there were two exactly half-inch
cubes of butter; equally exiguous portions of marmalade and
sugar; one cup full and one third of a cup of coffee in the pot;
three thin halves of toast; no bread. I wondered how many of
the audience, liberally sprinkled with Indian, Thai, Chinese
and other foreign students, at the previous evening's rumbus-
tious performance of *Tom Jones* by the Oxford Players,
endured with good grace similar near-privations. Luckily
there were cheap, really cheap new eating-places where
owners of appetites, more robust than the oriental, paid daily
levy. I joined them in sympathy.

Oxford is one of those places which encourage the art of valediction. There is something about Carfax, the Turl, the Broad and the High and Cornmarket, that mixture of din and sudden quiet, of business mart and 'grove of academe', the flourish of stylish outfitters' showrooms coupled with the flurry of posters of esoteric societies on college screens which is too 'Compton Mackenzie' to be surrendered to more than once in a lifetime. If one were not careful to go now and leave youth to youth, one might almost be tempted to stay on and on, until one of those damp November dusks when 'the darkness and fog slowly blot out St John's and the alley of elm-trees opposite, and give to the Martyrs' Memorial and even to Balliol a gothic and significant mystery'. Then Oxford, the university, is a city within a city, where, outside, present life manifests its continuity, and inside lighted rooms 'the battles and the glories, the thoughts, the theories and the speculations of the past move across printed pages' (Compton Mackenzie, *Sinister Street*).

Oxford is a city within a city in another sense also. To the Victorian idealist it was the English city which provided the clearest idea of the feudal city of the Middle Ages; its towers and gardens, its dreaming spires gave the strongest possible contrast to the mills and smoking chimneys of a Leeds or Manchester or Birmingham. After the railway came, however, and the deplorable railway station, it was Victorian speculative builders who set the ancient city in its unattractive frame of brick, bringing villa-dom to its approaches and making of north Oxford 'perhaps the most quintessentially Victorian of all England's suburbs' (Asa Briggs). As I went out through it, on the road towards Witney, it seemed an element no less destructive to the Oxford 'dream' than the suburb of Cowley, agent of the automobile age which has subsequently played havoc with the Victorian pattern of cities.

Of the A40 to Witney the dominant traits were those of any trunk road, filling stations, fast traffic, smooth inclines, contrived to look almost level on deceptively rising curves, urgency for the cyclist—to get on and get off it. The blanket town of Witney itself fortunately lies off the highway. It is also fortunate in having its manufactory discreetly hidden and new estates separately grouped and planned, so that the pleasant Oxfordshire countryside still appears to environ the old market town. I enjoyed the warm stone group of Town Hall and seventeenth-century Butter Cross—a small structure on stone pillars with a gabled loft above; the buildings of the old grammar school dating from 1663; the spacious green at the head of the town, with its contrast of unhurried leisure after the bustle of the sloping, tree-shaded shopping street; the old houses leading to the bridge over the Windrush. Though not of the Cotswolds, topographically, Witney comes within the limestone belt and provides an agreeable appetiser to the real thing.

The hilltop road from there to Burford kept the Windrush valley in view, slightly hazed by mist, and led past Minster Lovell to the top of that celebrated town. Probably no part of the country is more often considered or acclaimed as the cream of England, or so considers and acclaims itself, than the Cotswolds. 'Within easy reach by car' is said of this range of hills by the guidebook of every inland watering-place and shopping centre in a radius of fifty or sixty miles—which is not, by any means, entirely to the Cotswolds' advantage. The towns and villages, whether they crown the tops or lie hidden among the folds of these hills, have had superimposed, it seems, as much 'twee-ness' and knick-knackery as the cottage rooms I used at Lechlade, whereas their real charm could best be revealed unadorned. For this the main reason has undoubtedly been that telling phrase 'within easy reach by car' and all the gimmickry that commercial exploitation nowadays adds to accessibility as a resort. For me, in consequence, some of the Cotswold cream curdled.

Burford, still in Oxfordshire, is of the Cotswolds in their south-eastern limits: the view of the High Street from its upper end would have been justification almost in itself of a Cotswold 'cream' claim—if only I could have seen it. What the accretions of the tourist-catching trade did not cover with their veneer of sameness, a double row of parked cars contrived almost completely to mask. The long, wide stone street with its pollarded limes, descending gently to the low-arched bridge over the Windrush, needs to be caught unawares, before 'tin man in his motor can' is about. Of course, a closer look at individual shops, houses and coaching inns (sign of Burford's revived source of prosperity), with one eye shut to the arty-craftiness of the generality, is rewarding. Cotswold stone and the vernacular of local building style have seen to that. Even when restored and modernised, most of this town's older premises reveal the Elizabethan style, which continued here long after the Elizabethan period itself—with dormer windows, gables, steep-pitched roofs covered with stone slates, Tudor windows with transoms, mullions and deep mouldings —because it was suitable for the building material of the local quarries and local conditions. In larger houses the dormers are finished with carved copings, finials and stone-slate verges, providing individuality and a decorative contrast to the massive simplicity of stone chimney-stacks. The fact that this whole area had formerly been rich in monasteries and religious houses meant, after the Dissolution, that large numbers of stonemasons and their apprentices were free to turn their skills to such domestic building, in both town and village, with the manifest benefits of detail and finish.

To see the Cotswold vernacular untrammelled and unvitiated and the effect of it in close-knit units like those of an estate village, I cycled over the Windrush bridge and out along its gentle open valley to Taynton, the Bonningtons, Windrush itself and back. In Taynton some cottage roofs have thatch instead of stone slates, but a fine group of farm and farm buildings show the vernacular at its best. Here are

The barns and comely manors planned
 By men who somehow moved in comely thought:
Who, with a simple shippon to their hand,
 As men upon some godlike business wrought.
(Drinkwater: 'The Midlands')

The late Renaissance mansion of Barrington Park, the churches and cottages of the two villages, clearly came from the same local quarries and have become an inevitable part of the 'soft surrounding scene' with their warm, lichen-covered stone. Windrush church and its tombstones leave no doubt that this country, if not especially Burford, owed its main prosperity to sheep and wool. From the solitary ram's head in the arcading to the heads of sheep, instead of the conventional cherubs, and their horns worked in with the fluted shell edges on the box tombs, they stand out distinctly.

The Cotswold cult dates from the 1920s and the appreciation of its vernacular, in the first place, stems largely from William Morris and the wide circle of artists, craftsmen and writers associated with him. Craftsmen, artists, writers still instinctively 'home' there—apart from those who fill the Burford shops with Welsh woollens, hand-thrown pots, hand-wrought iron, illuminated glass and the like. Christopher Fry, I discovered, lived at a village nearby: his brother was running a bookshop, tucked away in a courtyard, and he turned up for me some of the playwright's surplus books. (A disadvantage of cycle touring is that one comes across memorabilia of all kinds, but can seldom transport them. I missed acquiring an early Derby teapot, at a low figure, and an old native Indian brass tray for that reason: perhaps wisely I had admired the alabaster figure of Buddha in Lechlade only in shop-closing hours.)

Another Burford colonist I knew of already, *The Country-man*. But I had not known that its offices in Sheep Street were formerly the premises of a temperance hotel. The present editor, as he told me, had first come to the Cotswolds on a bicycle, as a boy, up from Devon, sleeping under the summer hedges and sometimes getting drenched. He showed me, with some satisfaction, a sepia photograph of the old temperance hotel on which was prominently displayed the sign of the CTC.

After my chutney-and-cheese sandwiches in the garden of the White Horse, with a view over Burford roofs and of the backs of buildings which have remained unchanged even when their fronts have been modified—I looked again at the Windrush bridge, the charming house adjacent and the parish church close by. Solid dignified tombs, some with representations of corded wool bales on top, others with renaissance ornament of skulls, bones, hour-glass, fill the churchyard. Within the church are memorials of every kind, from fifteenth-century brasses to the great lord of the manor's (and Lord Chief Justice's) monument that overshadows all others. For these rather than for the fabric itself the church is remarkable ... Then the road again, up Fulbrook Hill and on towards Chipping Norton, in a hazy-sun-warmed afternoon.

Any considerable relics of the ancient Forest of Wychwood, of which Shipton, a few miles further on, and its neighbours Milton and Ascot-under-Wychwood are reminders, lie further to the east in the vicinity of Charlbury. The dominant feature, mid-route, was the Evenlode valley, which runs down from Moreton-in-the-Marsh. I was glancing along its sinuous course, recalling the villages a little further up that Edward Thomas unforgettably evoked, after a fleeting glimpse from the train:

> *Yes. I remember Adlestrop—*
> *The name ...*

and the moment he described when, among willows, willow-herb and grass and meadowsweet,

> *a blackbird sang*
> *Close by: and round him, mistier,*
> *Farther and farther, all the birds*
> *Of Oxfordshire and Gloucestershire*
> ('Adlestrop')

—and the least expected happened. Softening, slurring, then gently hissing and finally bumping, 'Claud's' back tyre went flat. I came back from Edward Thomas and Adlestrop—where the steam hissed, as the express train drew up there unexpectedly that June afternoon—and set about examining it. As was soon evident, a bit of Cotswold flint had worked its

Page 107 (above) The 'Gateway to the Cotswolds'—the beautiful tree-lined High Street of Burford, Oxfordshire, backed by its picturesque stone-built houses and shops; (below) Little Rollright, near Chipping Norton

Page 108 (above) Stow-on-the-Wold with its village stocks on the
green. This is one of the few Cotswold villages built on a hill top;
(below) High Street, Tewkesbury, Gloucestershire

way through the defences of my 1¼in Michelin sports tyre.

After its repair, the last few miles to Chipping Norton (Old English *chipping*, Anglo-Saxon *cheapen* = market) seemed more laboured than usual, even allowing for the upland wind. But when I arrived there I was lucky in two things: there was a cycle shop—which in small towns nowadays is certainly not odds-on. Expert scrutiny brought to light a wearing cotter pin, which I had replaced, a less than tight spindle and a tendency for the rear wheel to run out of true again, for which the right wrench in the right hands soon provided cure. I asked the shop-owner what were the chances of bed and breakfast thereabouts. He named a few inns which might take a single, if they were not full, and failing that gave me the address of a private house, that of his sister-in-law. The inns were full—or did not think fit to let a double room for one bed—and so I had my second piece of luck. The Victorian house in Rock Street gave away nothing from the outside, but when I asked whether accommodation was available I was shown upstairs to a small back bedroom almost completely filled by its bed.

Not that the room was particularly small, but the bed was enormous—a large double four-poster, whose canopy reached the ceiling and whose solid oak columns had bulbous swellings as big as footballs. Its head and footboard were heavily carved in seventeenth-century style, while a panel in the headboard opened to reveal a 'priest-hole' or two-compartment cupboard. The accredited date of this monster was 1640 (it had been acquired at a Sheffield sale some thirty years before): the only similar one known to the owner was in a state room at Chastleton House. Five men, I learnt, had staggered upstairs under the weight of the solid headboard alone when it was being installed in its present home. I pondered on the weight of the canopy which loomed darkly above on those massive columns—but, even so, jumped at the chance of sleeping in Jacobean splendour for a night.

The effects of the Cotswold industry, tourism, were not so self-evident at Chipping Norton as at some other places. Of

Bourton-on-the-Water and of Broadway I was to hear even 'Cotsallers' themselves express distaste. Some writers on the Cotswolds exclude this town on the eastern fringe altogether, although it is certainly within the same oolite belt and shares building characteristics—which fact perhaps goes some way to explain its naturalness. I savoured the creamy-golden stone buildings of High Street and Middle Street, linked on its lower level by shallow steps, and the uniform dignified façades of the larger houses, hotels and banks in comparatively uncluttered state. The market-place has a seventeenth-century inn and almshouses and the classical market-hall by G. S. Repton stands up boldly. The old school buildings on the hill-slope lead the eye beyond to a wide sweep of swelling upland: a pinnacled and turreted nineteenth-century tweed mill declares this wool town's later source of employment. Chipping Norton is coherent, all of a piece: the cottages flush to the pavement on the outskirts have the same satisfying lines and stone honesty as the big houses nearer the centre.

After my evening meal—a 'scratch' but generous one of salad, fresh vegetables, tinned salmon, bread and butter and fruit laid out in the Victorian dining-room, with its weeping-willow-and-stone-urn outlook—at Rock Street, my landlady chatted about her own cycling days and youthful eagerness to explore England, and from that went on to the subject of her children and *their* activities. At weekends and holidays, she complained, they would lie abed until all hours if not forced out. They had not always been like that. It was part of the change, the noticeable slackness and indifference that had come over them, teenage grammar school girls, once keen, interested and willing to work, since the time they had been forced to attend the comprehensive school. Education, in their view, now, was not worth while, going to University simply a waste of time. Their present school's tone, it appeared, was mainly set with the aid of a pupil committee and co-operation with its suggestions. Encouragement to the academically able to become more able, much less outstanding, was not the policy. Staff were mainly young, mini-skirted, lax on discipline and unconcerned with homework. The few of better calibre soon left for schools in Oxford or elsewhere.

How could one swim, asked my landlady, against this sluggish stream, these slack standards, this attitude of anything-will-do-for-country-children? She was disheartened, her husband equally so, but apprehensive about the prospects of his own job under the local authority, if he spoke out. One was left to wonder, and to wonder how many parents felt the same in Chipping Norton and other comprehensified places.

*   *   *

I left next morning in a hazy sunshine that flattered the town's timeless stone, by the minor road to Churchill, the Evenlode valley and Bledington. A great acreage of cornland unfolded, with substantial farms, converted watermills, houses with the country-gentlemanly air that comes almost automatically when they are larger than cottages in these parts, and inns setting their caps at a clientèle looking for steak bars and bistros. Wary now of Cotswold flints, I kept well away from verges and took the first undulating few miles a little gingerly on the repaired tyre, to test it out. A dead stoat and a few ditch-walking pheasants were the only hazards.

Stow-on-the-Wold lifted ahead from valley level, at 300 feet, to almost 800 feet. The oldest of the three hilltop towns on or near the Fosse Way—the others are Northleach and Moreton-in-the-Marsh—Stow was on the line of a Cotswold ridgeway route that existed well before Roman times. Always a place of call for travellers, and a market town for the surrounding villages and farms, it manifestly sets out to attract the passing motorist. The picturesquely beautiful town, that grew up about the wide market-place, with small alley-ways leading off and a small town hall at centre, is not quite, but very nearly submerged in the tittivated tourist-trap. Brightly coloured paint, that shouts against the old grey stone, attracts attention to the new cafés and hotels and studios. 'Angela's Styles', 'Deborah's Kitchen', 'Coppers' tea-room and the various galleries of expensive antiques and crafts set the tone. Lady painters hail each other in ringing tones, large florid men with carefully-kept long white hair, red sweaters and white trousers catch, as they mean to do, the visitor's eye. The place is busy, cafés and shops often crowded, but empty of true small-town feeling. The cars and coaches and their over-spill distract one from the handsome details—such as St Edward's House in the Square, with its fluted pilasters, niched doorway and shallow rise of steps.

Dropping down again from Stow to Upper Swell on the Dikler (a tributary of the Windrush) I passed a group of cyclist-campers ensconced on the wide grass verge. They had chosen an effectively sheltered place to dispose their tents, in the lee of the great park wall of 'Abbotswood'—and had within eye-shot a charming village. The stone bridge over the river, the mill, the houses and cottages grouped about the late Tudor manor-house, the diminutive church with its Norman south doorway form here a well-mannered, harmonious group. From there on, apart from a solitary roadside farm, the way was completely bare in the sparse, rolling Cotswold style of upland landscape, until I reached Ford, near Cutsdean.

> *Ye weary travellers that pass by*
> *With dust and scorching sunbeams dry*
> *Or be ye numbed with snow and frost*
> *With having these bleak Cotswolds crost*
> *Step in and quaff my nut brown ale*
> *Bright as rubys mild and stale*
> *Twill make your lagging trotters dance*
> *As nimble as the suns [sons?] of France*
> *Then will ye own ye men of sense*
> *That neare [ne'er?] has better spent sixpence.*

This sign of the Plough Inn was compelling even in lesser extremes of weather. With a mug of rough cider and a ham roll I sat on a bench in the stone-flagged yard, in sun, among kittens, sleek bitches and the sound of ponies from a stable half-door. Only a dairyman and a girl carrying a bridle came by me while I enjoyed for half an hour this quiet heart-country of the Cotswolds, under the slope of Cutsdean Hill and near Buckle Street or Buggildway, a prehistoric track-way running north to south along the hills.

As piquant contrast in this area of the north Cotswolds I should have liked to have been able to visit Sezincote, on the other side of Bourton Down. The opposite in every way to 'vernacular style', it is an oriental domed house, in the Brighton Pavilion sense (and also designed by Repton) in a Hindu setting of great cedars and garden temples, willow-fringed lakes, bridges decorated with sacred bulls and elephants: it was built for a retired high official of the East India Company. A touch of the exotic here would have been welcome—but for the tyrant *road*. For although the Cotswolds provide a good example of man's ability to harmonise with the beauty of natural surroundings, indeed to enrich it, these gentle uplands studded with near-perfect small towns and villages nearly all made of the same yellowy limestone tend to cloy, if unrelieved.

The Cycling Bureau, as I learned later, together with the Council for the Protection of Rural England, has made recent efforts to trace out those miles of unspoilt countryside which can best be seen from a bicycle. As cycle route of the year (1972) they selected a thirty-eight-mile route in the Cotswolds, worked out by Vice-Admiral Sir Ian Campbell. To any tourist who embarks on this I would recommend the next few miles as valediction . . . From Ford, leaving the by-road to Temple Guiting, site once of a small preceptory of the Templars and later of the most perfect of Tudor houses, the way continues over finely sculptured wold, with dips of wooded valley, to a final height of 840 feet at Stumps Cross. Then, abruptly, off the edge of the uplands and by long sweeping curves, one glides in one glorious descent down to Stanway and the plain. Glimpsed ahead, as the bicycle swings round almost hairpin bends, lies a new landscape and a reach of country from Gloucestershire across the Severn valley and to Hereford. The change is complete, the descent mildly sensational and the height of the Cotswolds dramatically revealed.

From the bare folds and cool hazy atmosphere of these uplands my road now led, in mild sunshine with views of the bosky hogsback of Bredon Hill, by Alderton and Aston Cross to Tewkesbury. After uniform Cotswold stone and its mannered perfection, the mixture of black-and-white buildings, brick-and-timber houses, flower-decorated cottages leading to the waterside and the bustle of ordinary shopping streets seemed like re-entering reality after leaving a carefully preserved showpiece. The great Norman tower of the Abbey in warm reddish stone, 'comparable with the best found anywhere in southern England' (*Shell Guide to England*), and the old clap-board mill almost in its shadow, lend distinction to this approach to Tewkesbury from the south and east.

The town unfolds on a traffic-thronged thoroughfare, with many old houses and inns, in fact something of almost every architectural style since the Elizabethan era. The inns include the Hop Pole with a fourteenth-century fireplace, before which Mr Pickwick warmed his coat tails, and the Tudor House with a priest-hole proper in one of the chimneys. The Black Bear, at the top of the High Street, has built into it part of a bridge over the Avon, before its confluence with the Severn, and is said to date from *c* 1200. With such houses as that of the Nodding Gables, ancient wooden-panelled shops and their overhanging eaves, with all the intriguing passageways and alleys that lead off towards the river or into bright flower gardens just behind the three main streets, I found the afternoon consuming itself without any mileage being added. Tewkesbury centre, protected by conservation order, if freed from traffic, would have kept me still longer. A vast ship's or factory boiler, almost as wide as the carriageway, that came rumbling through on its transporter nearly forced cyclist and pedestrians alike into the wall. After Cotswold quiet even the noise was offensive. I turned my wheel again towards quieter places and crossed Tewkesbury's other bridge, Telford s graceful iron span across the Severn.

When I turned off the Ledbury road towards Upton-on-Severn I was not thinking yet of the night's resting-place. This first pleasant taste of Worcestershire's orchard and farmland in the mellow early evening light gave appetite for more. But, on the unfenced lawn of a light-blue-and-white painted clap-boarded house, set among apple trees, I chanced to notice a small sign. Being 'open to accident' I inquired about the accommodation. The young couple, it appeared, had only been installed a couple of weeks at 'By-the-Way', the B & B sign of the former occupant had not yet been taken down. They had not thought out the pros and cons of doing beds and meals, but if I liked to look at the only room that was reasonably straight . . . And so, on a by-road, in a preservation area, with a view across to the Malverns and 'Claud' in the conservatory of what had originally been a gentleman's summer residence, I settled for pot luck—'when my husband comes home from the office in Cheltenham'. It and breakfast also were almost worthy of Egon Ronay mention: my only regret was that the local, a few yards down the road, preferred to 'keep out of trouble' by not keeping cider on draught. The same cry meets one almost everywhere as one reaches cider country—or is it too inexpensive for publicans nowadays to bother?

> Bienvenu à Upton-upon-Severn nichée entre les collines de Malvern et celles de Cotswolds. Elle est une ville du long passé historique, batie sur les bords de la Severn qui coule vers Gloucester en traversant un paysage de plaines fertiles et de jardins coquets.

From the town guide's welcome to visitors in Common Market terms, this factually sums up its appeal. It has one long street, agreeably diversified with houses ranging from early Tudor to early Victorian, some timber-framed inns and the scatter of antique shops usual in this backward-looking era in even smaller places of resort. I admired the three-storied stuccoed White Lion, with its huge pilasters and porch and heraldic beast atop: it was used as a setting by Fielding in

Tom Jones. The two fine Georgian houses near the river front command attention, but at this time of year Upton's chief attraction, its busy boating scene, was left to the imagination. From here one can cruise by Severn and Avon to the centre of Evesham, among those pleasant 'plaines fertiles et jardins coquets'.

My morning's aim was the Malverns, strung across the slope of their hills apparently just across the river. As I came over the level against a stiff westerly breeze they seemed at first to be retreating instead of getting nearer. The last rise was deceptive too, seemingly slight and easy until one realised that at their high point the Malvern Hills reach 1,395 feet. Villas, prep schools, an empty hotel, gardens with views across to the Vale of Evesham, tree-shaded walks, then the Abbey appeared.

'That's what I like to see,' said a voice at my elbow as I pulled up by the Mount Pleasant, Great Malvern. 'Doing it yourself, not by combustion. How far are you going?'

I told him—all the way round. The speaker was a warden of the Malvern Hills, another former cyclist who regretted that he had given it up. He had thought nothing once of pedalling away to Cornwall, but now had to be content with patrolling the ten-mile stretch of the home range. His vigorous carriage and open-air complexion left no doubt that this was the next best thing. But it was the freedom of the wheel that he missed.

Malvern on a sunny morning is an easy place to loiter in. I looked from the garden terrace of Mount Pleasant Hotel, in front of its eighteenth-century orangery, across to the creeper-swathed frontage of the Priory Hotel, to the green enclosure and massive, decorated tower of the Abbey, to the College and to the blue distance far beyond. There was little else perhaps of grandeur or distinction, but much accumulation of picturesque detail, chiefly Victorian. Malvern, terraced on its hill slope, shows to advantage the medley of its roof features—domes, belfries, spires, turrets, belvederes—in neo-Gothic style, the amusing superfluities of a prosperous era of growth, when the water cure was at the height of popularity, grafted on to villas and boarding-houses set among the still traceable premises of its older hotels, library and pump room. One of the major hotels even now carries a sign about the departure times of mail coaches: but the steep road to St Ann's Well, taken by the 'waterers', is punctuated by antiques, boutiques and tea-rooms.

Despite the penumbra of the select colleges and schools—Malvern Girls' College, on its application form for entrants, asks 'through whom introduced', 'father's and mother's initials, surname, title and decorations', offers boarding places at £300 per term, exclusive of such extras as books, music and speech or riding lessons—there is an intimate, almost home-grown atmosphere about this spa town. Even a certain rich eccentricity—as in the railway station, which, I was amused to find, has astonishingly realistic capitals to its cast-iron platform pillars, incorporating chestnuts, lilies, strawberries both wild and domestic, oakleaves and daisies in their diverse designs and in full colour. A claim, made in the Information Bureau, that Malvern is 'the premier inland resort of England' relies, surely, more on the environment and the festival attractions of music and drama than on the urbanity of the town itself. The centre is small, limiting, awkward in site and, as I saw on leaving via North Malvern, its tailing off to ordinariness is marked, even in contrast to lesser places like Upton. Artisan pubs and artisan cottages of a kind not to be found in Woodhall Spa belong here.

Among up-and-down lanes, pockets of woodland, apple orchards and trellised hopfields I swung away from North Hill to Storridge and Stifford's Bridge. Oasthouses landmarked some of the farms, others stood out magpie-fashion in their white and black at the head of rolling green fields. Roadside pubs had their signs again, NO GIPSIES OR TRAVELLERS, and farm gates CALLERS ONLY BY ARRANGEMENT. In summer there would be encampments in quiet lanes and hoppickers and their families and their dogs everywhere. A blue sky and high white cumulus emphasised the richness of this

Worcester–Hereford border country, the 'coloured counties', sometimes of almost Rhineland appearance. I sought lanes quieter than the A4103 (Worcester–Hereford) and came by sudden dips and swings to Suckley and Linley Green. From a wide gorse common overlooking the river Frome there were views as far as the Black Mountains of Brecknockshire and just down the road ahead the clustered plateau town of Bromyard.

This smallest of Hereford's market towns is a place easily overlooked, being left on one side by the trunk road from Worcester to Wales. In its two or three Rip-Van-Winklish streets there are some good black-and-white Elizabethan houses, one with diagonal bracing, a pub with a period steam engine on its sign called the Railway Arms, Dumbleton Hall which sports a splendid brass lion knocker, an Elizabethan grammar school and the least obvious of market-places. Tower Hill House across the way sheltered Charles I for the night of 3 September 1644. The town has an air of having waited ever since for something else of note to happen. The back lanes with saddlers and chandlers and scrap-iron yards soon lead off into unmade roads at the fringe and a new housing estate.

There was really nothing to stay longer for, I thought, after I had looked about—until I spotted a B & B sign in front of the Congregational Chapel. Inconspicuous outside, the chapel was plain within in the eighteenth-century way, with black wood pulpit and pews and distempered walls and brass lovingly maintained. Close behind it beyond an open vault, but surrounded by a neat kitchen garden and looking over the Frome, was the former manse. 'Yes', said the lady who answered the door, 'I do have accommodation for one and I'm just preparing supper. It's chicken: there'll be enough for another portion, I'm sure. Put your bike in the schoolroom there—mind the vault now—and come in. I get all sorts Canadians, Americans, Australians.'

So I stayed—but did not find out what it was that Bromyard awaited, or for what they all came.

Unusual names cropped up among the villages on the road next morning—Tedstone Wafer, Stoke Bliss, Hanley Child, Pensax, Neen Sollars, Laysters Pole—a touch perhaps of Welsh fancy, a kind of descant on the usually simple tunes of place nomenclature. Nothing quite as exotic as Britwell Salome or the Fifehead Magdalen, Ryme Intrinseca, Cricket Malherbie that I noted on the Somerset–Dorset borders, nor as suggestive as Plush, Folly and Droop in the same region, but a change from all the Nortons, Comptons, Astons and Shiptons of Gloucestershire. There were other novelties too. A roadside cottage in the merest hamlet, Kyre Magna, had a window full of Chinese figures and Newhall porcelain tea-bowls and saucers. A home-made sign, far too inconspicuous to halt a motorist in passage, indicated 'Antiques'. Inside the cottage there were the calf-bound relics of a gentleman's library, *Tristram Shandy,* with Hogarth's engravings, Smollett's *History of England,* sermons, natural histories and a bijou set of Alexander Pope. For once I took the bait of treasure trove by the wayside and came out with one pound less, but a neat pocket volume on British Poisonous Plants with thirty-six hand-coloured illustrations. I had not known before that the scent itself of some innocent-looking spring flowers, such as daffodils, was toxic—although I had known that some people were allergic to sap on their fingers from the cut stems.

In this country of little wooded hills and hopfields and rich tillage I rode easily along the course of a tributary of the Teme to Tenbury Wells. Once a spa also, patronised in the mid-nineteenth century for its saline springs, and a stopping-place then for coaches on the London–North Wales run, it still has agreeable reminders of those days in the timber-framed inns down Market Street and in the odd little Victorian-Gothic pump room, in a bit of wilderness near a trout stream. Its spires, gables and ogee windows, all in rusting sheet metal, now look down on the weekly cluster of Women's Institute stalls. There is also an unusual, round, brick-built market hall near the Cage Hotel, looking more like an auction-mart cattle-ring than a place to display vegetables, fruit, eggs, farm butter, hares, and pheasants in season. The late Norman tower of the parish church is a little way behind and less conspicuous. All in all, with its leisurely pace, its light-and-bright building styles and its medieval three-arched bridge over the Teme, which separates it from the busy Worcester road, Tenbury is the ideal place for a sunny morning and the study of small town *moeurs*.

'Nice to know there's another about on the road.' I turned from contemplating the Teme to the speaker beside me on the bridge.

'Yes . . . getting on for the third week now,' I said.

'Oh, been around a bit, have you? It was your bike, though, that I meant. Don't see so many Claud Butlers this way."

The by-now-usual tale: he had had his own 'Claud' in the fifties—one of the then ultra-lightweight road-racing models that weighed only 24lb fully equipped. When he gave up he had kept the frame, removing wheels and head-race, but not the bottom bracket. Only this year it had been reassembled, with the necessary replacements, and handed over to his son, aged sixteen, for a first tour to the Lake District.

'Just where I am going,' I said, 'if I don't run into trouble.'

'You won't—not on a Claud Butler . . . Well, then, cheerio.'

I enjoyed these Midland roads, with Clee Hill as steady landmark to the north, prosperous farms and market gardens to left and right, and the valley of the Teme drawing me into Shropshire. Undemanding, unspectacular, undisturbed country on to Little Hereford, Woofferton, Comberton, Richards Castle. The latter now has only the earthworks left of its pre-Conquest stronghold, but there is a seventeenth-century Court House, an old cider mill and dovecot of great, unknown age, while the church still has its seventeenth-century box pews and hatchments on the walls of one of the oldest families in Debrett, the Salways. Hereabouts torpor, not the febrile march of time, is the contagion one might have to fear.

Into the A 49's traffic—the main route from South Wales to Lancashire—for the last few miles and a tight squeeze among cattle trucks and diesel lorries in the narrow descent to hump-backed, single-line Ludford Bridge, at the foot of Ludlow. I left the ruck of traffic here to enter this beautiful town through Broadgate Arch and to walk up Broad Street, which has been called the finest street in England. From the black-and-white timbered front of the Angel—where Nelson was once a guest—along the broad pavement before faultless houses dating from the fourteenth and fifteenth centuries, up to the eighteenth-century buttercross (a columned and pedimented classical building designed as Town Hall) the prospect is wholly pleasing. Whether one turns left or right from the buttercross the eye is constantly held by vistas of great charm. If one forgets the newer, rather fierce red-brick market hall, a dignified frontage of girls' grammar school and old houses flanks the approach to the castle. Massively built, impressively large, splendidly sited on high ground partly encircled by the rivers Teme and Corve, even its remains would still seem capable of defying the Welsh marauders against whom it was erected. The Princes in the Tower knew it, so did Catherine of Aragon and Sir Philip Sidney; Prince Arthur, brother of Henry VII, died there; Milton's masque *Comus* was first performed within its walls. Today, at the summer festival, the inner bailey accommodates both actors and audience for a Shakespeare play. On Boxing Day a meet of the South Shropshire Hunt assembles within its walls and clatters by the gatehouse out through the town. The view of castle and town, spreading over the hill below it, and of the tower of the great church high over all, made descent to the river and climb up towards Mary Knoll opposite a worthwhile effort.

I found the Rose and Crown for a snack lunch, tucked away in a courtyard off Church Street, and first licensed in the sixteenth century, but tuned in now to scampi and sherry custom instead of 'scrumpy' and cheese. Just round the corner was a Tudor house with a three-storey Jacobean porch. All the back lanes here are picturesque, narrow and bustling, with old-clothes stores, fish-and-chip booths and vegetable stalls elbowed by audio-visual studios and Welsh craft displays in the modern manner. From the buttercross and the leaning black-and-white gable end opposite, the street opens into the Bull Ring. Here across the main stream of traffic stands one of England's finest half-timbered inns, beloved by American tourists, the seventeenth-century Feathers. Its timber work had recently been restored to the natural oak, so that it looked more than ever like a film set. The first selling price of this hostelry, whose dining room ceiling is embossed with a copy of the arms of James I, was £225; in 1947 it changed hands at £30,000 and just recently, I was told, had attracted an offer of £125,000 from a hotel syndicate. But the jaunty parade of mini-skirted shop girls through the Bull Ring, the hikers picnicking on the buttercross steps, the singsong voices of border country farmers and their wives, the knots of hobbledehoy country lads contribute to Ludlow's everyday atmosphere and help to counter the risk of its being turned into a mere showpiece.

Descending the hill from the Bull Ring, on the A 49, conscious all the way of buildings of quality and at its foot of an irregular row of timbered inns and houses that anywhere else would surely have been a prime attraction, I joined the thrusting stream towards Shrewsbury. The tower of the parish church, 135 feet higher than the castle, was a presence, glimpsed as I rounded the corner, that would dominate the view of this near-perfect town and neighbouring Bringewood Chase, as long as I cared or dared to look back. But the road had been recently straightened or was still in that speed-promoting process, with hamlets like Bromfield shrinking back from the threatening road and rumble, and not to keep one's eye on immediate surroundings was an obvious actuarial and gratuitous risk.

The outline of Brown Clee Hill, further north than Titterstone Clee, came into view, then the butt end of Wenlock Edge sheltering Corve Dale, and on the other side, first the hillocks that protect those 'quietest places under the sun', Clunton, Clunbury, Clungunford and Clun, then the nursery slopes of Long Mynd. I looked across at what appeared to be a castle in a churchyard: it was an embattled church tower standing side-by-side with one of England's earliest fortified manor-houses, Stokesay Castle, from which it is separated by the moat. Both are enhanced by the presence of a small mere. It was over the nearby river Onny that Telford set one of his smaller cast-iron bridges, but the new road had no use for that. Craven Arms came and went, a cattle mart centre formerly an important coach stop on the Welsh run: most of it is tucked away from view and shows (to through traffic) only its worst side, coal sidings, railwaymen's cottages, bus stops, a decaying cinema.

Until I reached Marshbrook the belts of woodland, plough and pasture, the sudden lift of hills beyond Hopedale were incidental to the job of watching my wheels and those of the 'heavy stuff'. Then, within a mile or so, all was peace. I left the 'bypass' for the village road to the Strettons, All, Church and Little, that hugs the edge of the Mynd. Fortunate places to have kept out of the mainstream and to have a 1,500-foot moorland barrier between them and westerly gales. Here it was almost like riding in a vacuum. Little Stretton with its old 'magpie' manor-house, clipped box arches to cottage gates, pub with outside tables and benches, and its unusual thatched black-and-white church—fairly modern, this—sits facing Ragdon Hill. At the other end of the group All Stretton strings one or two handsome houses, one square and Georgian, a country club and an old people's home along the road, whilst tucking its choicer cottages and bungalows back into the lee of Long Mynd.

Between these two villages lies 'town', Church Stretton, quite fashionable as a health resort at the end of the last century and developed then into a place of two shopping streets instead of the original one, with its minute market square. Church Stretton sits facing Caer Caradoc, rock-crowned 1,500-foot hill, and backs into the deep valley of Cardingmill, carved almost up to the spine of the Mynd. I liked the look of the half-timbered older street, a country mixture of drapers, ironmongers, doctor's surgery, almshouses, house agent, junk shop, clock repairer and pubs. Just behind it was the church, behind that the large, brick, eighteenth-century 'old rectory' and behind that a hanger of 'nature trail' woodland. After drawing blank at one pub—it was undergoing a refit —and finding another full, I noticed in a courtyard, lying against the wall, an old CTC sign. Here too until recently there had been a pub, the Raven, now without licence but willing still to provide bed and breakfast. So, almost at the hub of the town, with a seat among the family at breakfast and a bedroom view to Hope Bowdler and Ragdon Hill, I took here my Salopian ease. Fortunately the King's Head, though refitting, still did its soup, fish or steak, cheese and wine trade over the bar, where the house agent, half-hidden behind his beard and beer, kept a keen eye on newcomers.

Church Stretton's air of well-bred resignation and its apparent consciousness of being a town by-passed, consorted well with the dreamy quality of the evening scene. The rounded feminine slopes above Cardingmill, the masculine outcrops of Caradoc became almost luminous with a green-gold light, then changed to silvery and black, as a half-moon rose. In its pale radiance red-brick Sandford Avenue, the 'new' development, took on a temporary look: the old black-and-white street and tiny square assumed their old importance. On the outskirts, where a big hotel stood elephantine on its corner site, gutted and long left empty after a fire, and where large detached houses on pot-holed, unadopted roads, receded into thick fir woods, the reality of the place seemed to fade altogether. Not quite, but almost another Woodhall Spa—with a Catholic retreat, instead of a Kinema-in-the-Woods.

*　　　　　*　　　　　*

The Celtic, dream-like atmosphere lasted into the next day. I crossed Watling Street (A 49), climbed out of villa-dom towards Gaer Stone, jutting sentinel of Hope Dale, and entered a land of lost content, with the hamlets of Hope

Page 125 (above) Ludlow; (below) the English Bridge which spans the river Severn at Shrewsbury, Shropshire, and dates back to 1774

Page 126 (above) The Trough of Bowland, Lancashire; (below) the Lake District

Bowdler, Wall-under-Heywood, Longville-in-the-dale drows-
ing under the tree-hung wave of Wenlock Edge. From the
narrow ridgetop I could look back now to Brown Clee, then,
on the other side through a leafy screen across the pattern of
fields and farms, wood and water-meadows far below towards
Plaish, Holt and Church Preen—a secret-looking, remote
Mary Webb country. (She actually honeymooned in Church
Stretton.) Beyond Wilderhope—evocative name—on the edge
of Easthope Wood, a gap in the trees and a precipitous pitch
of crag allowed one to look down, almost suspended in space,
from the escarpment over the whole region and its long-
abandoned grass-grown railway track. A land, one might
believe, of old ways and older memories, of life tranquil—or
unbearably stagnant—as one took it. Certainly there was a
slow-moving, friendly tempo about the people, with hidden
moods, no doubt, that set both Mary Webb's and Housman's
imagination working when 'the woods were in riot and the
gale of life blew high':

> ... before my time the Roman
> At yonder heaving hill would stare,
> The blood that warms an English yeoman,
> The thoughts that hurt him, they were there.

('On Wenlock Edge the wood's in trouble')

I rode on, for a time past modern manifestations, lime
quarries, a garden sculpture manufactory, a water-logged
dump of old cars, and into the outskirts of Much Wenlock.
The dream was scarcely broken. This miniature market town
appears to have had only superficial changes for several centuries and preserves in parts a medieval character. The High
Street, beginning with a Georgian hotel as token of up-to-
dateness, soon becomes a narrow thoroughfare of overhanging
gables, black timbered inns, venerable houses with carved
shutters, a stone-built cornmarket, and ends, at the Cross, in
the old Guildhall. The latter is constructed on the oak arches
of a butter market (still used), and its wooden upper storey,
rich in carvings, dated 1577, acts as court room and council

chamber. Picturesque houses and old shop premises abound: just beyond those on the left of Guildhall stands Wenlock's unique attraction.

In this, the eleventh-century Cluniac priory, time recedes effortlessly into a dateless past—on green turf among fair gardens, between the crumbling walls of the chapter house, with their pattern of interlaced Norman arches, surrounded by broken columns, sculptured figures, fragments of the monks' lavatory. Before its priory days there was a convent here, built at the urgency of Lady Godiva: before that and destruction by the Danes a seventh-century foundation of St Milburga. Beside it even the fifteenth-century house near St Owen's Well begins to seem modern.

Within less than five miles I came to a place as different from Much Wenlock as meths from mead and one that seemed scarcely to belong in Shropshire. Over the tail end of Wenlock Edge, past the lane to Homer and oddly called 'Wigwig', into a wooded gorge guarded by square stone lodges with black-and-white window shutters in the Welsh style, then by the entrance to Buildwas Abbey and I was crossing the Severn on what remains of Telford's first cast iron bridge, produced by the Coalbrookdale Company. As a large surviving casting built into the newer structure reveals, it was erected in 1796. For at Coalbrookdale ironworks, a mile or two beyond, had begun the process which was to change the face of northern England—the smelting of iron from coke instead of from the rapidly dwindling supplies of charcoal. It soon made coal the magnet of industry everywhere, and has left its enduring memorials in this 'cradle of the Industrial Revolution'.

At Ironbridge, a little further down the Severn past the cooling towers and huge chimney of a modern power station —visible even on Long Mynd—I came to the famous archetype of iron bridges, built in 1779 by Abraham Darby to cross the river in a single 100-foot span, 40 feet high and weighing 378 tons. This graceful and oldest of iron bridges faces the Tontine Hotel and when after crossing it on foot (it has been closed to vehicular traffic since 1934) one looks back to the hotel entrance one sees why: the warping of its structure with the passage of 194 years and the remorseless inward pressures of the steep river banks becomes alarmingly clear. At its base in a workshop at the rear of a cottage are the surviving relics of another trade, more ancient than that of ironmasters—those of a coracle-builder. The 'green' frame and laths, the calico cover and coat of pitch that made these Severn craft are going the way of most rural relics, but miniature coracles may still be had. After watching for a while the luck of those fishing from the bridge piers or from punts in the stream I took a drink at the Station Hotel on the far side. 'Station', of course, is another superannuated relic, since the line has closed and its halls and platforms crumbled, but there was over the bar a fine coloured engraving of the bridge and a china plate with a sepia transfer print of its span.

Apart from the dignified brick presence of the Tontine, the matching brick Market Hall with its five blank arches and pediment, and the blackened tower of St Luke's overhead, at the top of a hundred steep steps, Ironbridge had the atmosphere, rather sad, despoiled, anachronistic of a place that prosperity has passed by. Its old shops and narrow main street of cottages were in process of demolition, the back lane climbing the hill to better houses looked over the Severn gorge across raw gaps. Despite the cooling towers, its situation could be turned to great advantage: its air of dereliction may be only temporary. I was tempted instead to follow the river down to Coalport Bridge, another ornate cast-iron structure, carrying its name and date, 1818, as centre-piece. The rails, protected by prosaic modern scaffolding, were formed in a poetic pattern of concentric circles and cross-pieces, all in iron. Over the half-door of the minute toll-house, on the bridge approach, one could glimpse an elaborate, old-fashioned fire range rich with fleur-de-lys and other emblems —also cast-iron.

At Coalport's eighteenth-century pottery—not producing ceramics today—one or two of the old bottle kilns were still

in situ and the remaining structure of the pottery at Jack-
field was visible on the opposite bank. The whole area invited
one to linger and dig deeper into the survivals of a great
inventive era, picking up from some workman's cottage per-
chance a piece of Coalport porcelain decorated by Billingsley.
But my road led uphill from Severn's banks, past the Dunge
and Brosely crossroads, by Barrow and the race course and so
to complete the loop at Much Wenlock.

Under the influence of Wenlock air I turned my wheel
again, back past the barber's-cum-old-coin-and-clock shop,
past the Georgian hotel and on to Wenlock Edge. I took a
bite and sup on top at the Plough, where 'Old Fred', a farmer
with a figure like a Toby jug and a ten-gallon gabardine hat,
was propounding his opinion about weather signs. At the end
of a long dry spell when the springs have almost dried up it
was his belief that they flood again *before* a change to storm
and rain. Then I descended into the land of lost content to
seek out an old friend's house. He was in the garden, making
a 'Capability' landscape out of a bit of wilderness, and forth-
with I was in for a night's 'proud Salopian' hospitality.

*   *   *

> You will derive benefit from cycling so long as you keep
> within your natural physical capabilities, but never put in a
> straining spirit even though there be a man behind ... If
> you cannot ride a hill without opening your mouth get off
> and walk ... Never continue level road riding when you
> feel it a strain. This causes irregularity of the heart action
> and may be otherwise injurious ... Twopenny worth of
> claret mixed with a bottle of lemonade is a good thirst
> quencher. A plan which will be found excellent to *prevent*
> thirst while riding is to keep a short piece of quill (part of
> an old quill pen) in the mouth like a cigarette. This draws
> fresh air but compels the lips to be closed, so no dust gets
> into the mouth to make it dry ... Don't cycle with a whistle
> in your mouth as verdigris forms and may lead to poisoning.

A 'handy hint' presumably addressed to the captain on a
'whistle-stop' club outing.

Not all of these tips for turn-of-the-century cyclists are as comic, perhaps, as they now sound—at any rate for the 'beginner-again', who was also advised:

> Cyclists out of practice will find they can accomplish a journey with much greater ease and comfort if they rest a little after the first two miles.

Morning broke in sparkling mood. Two full-grown brown hares were sitting up on the edge of the 'wilderness' boxing, moving round each other to spar, as if in a ring. At times just their ears were visible, like RDF antennae, above the longish grass. When I resumed my way northward, along Watling Street, I noticed something else. Or rather the absence of something—wind. If there was any at all it came lightly from the south-west. Another normal element was missing too— traffic. As the day was Sunday the heavy lorry stuff had not taken over the road and there were as yet few cars about. It was the right sort of day for an effort—especially after my easy 'potter' of the previous one.

I followed the old Roman road, which from All Stretton onwards runs parallel to the A 49 under the slopes of Caer Caradoc and the Lawley, until it reaches Longnor Green. Then it begins to veer away in the direction of Wroxeter (Uriconium) and there I left it and the company of isolated farms, hazel hedges, watersplash crossings, snug estate cottages and the diminishing skyline of Long Mynd, for Ryton, Condover of the handsome, creamy-pink stone sixteenth-century Hall and the main Shrewsbury road. With the Wrekin in blue outline away to the right and the tall spires of Shrewsbury pointing ahead, I was running down from Bayston Hill to English Bridge in no time.

On any other day but Sunday a stop in Shrewsbury would have been irresistible—if only to explore streets with such names as Wyle Cop, Mardol, Dogpole, Shoplatch, Frankwell, the Dana, along with the old alleys Gullet Passage and Grope Lane, that have changed little since the time of Elizabeth I.

Instead I skirted the town centre by way of Murivance, along the line of the old walls, with a glimpse of the great public school (famed for its rowing) across the river, and by the unusual circular church of St Chad's. Dropping down to river-level at Welsh Bridge I continued along it until I linked up with the A 49 again. There is a choice of roads north to Whitchurch, by the A 49 or by a branch from it that leads through Wem. With a built-in leaning to lesser traffic routes, I followed the branch. So I enjoyed the quietest of country ways to Albrighton, Harmerhill and Alderton with a chance to take offside views at the dramatic pitch of Pontesbury Hill, at Breidden Hill near Welshpool and the more distant ridge of Stiperstones. I came to Wem just in time for Sunday 'opening'.

A somewhat puzzling town, Wem, famous for its ales and sometimes also remembered as boyhood home of William Hazlitt, whose little white house is in Noble Street. 'Bloody' Judge Jeffreys also lived there, at Lowe Hall, and took 'of Wem' for his barony title. After my shandy—6p again—and sandwich at a pub on the outskirts, and finding little else to delay for, I continued towards Whitchurch. At least, so I believed. When a couple of miles down Lovers Lane a branch signpost indicated Loppington and Oswestry, I began to wonder. By the map it seemed all wrong. No good letting Lovers Lane lead me on in another Celtic dream. So I went back to Wem main street, found the sign to Whitchurch and started afresh. Within a couple of miles I was back at the sign to Loppington. 'Yes', said the driver of a pulled-up van, 'it is the road to Whitchurch all right, not the direct one though.'

This time I let the road lead. A rainstorm suddenly blew up: visibility for a cyclist wearing glasses was limited. I seemed to be travelling from nowhere to nowhere—and what a deal of rural England there still is where one could say that between the conurbations. Through a hamlet or two, past lodge gates, alongside a canal, over a level crossing, into a blackly shining street and undoubtedly, if not 'directly', I had reached Whitchurch. The rain promptly ceased and I walked up the main street of a pleasant mellow market town (by-passed by through traffic) to the church of St Alkmund. Built originally of white stone—whence the name of the town —it collapsed early in the eighteenth century and was replaced by a classic building with a cupola, whose warm tones contrast well with the black-and-white frontages of shops close by.

So back again to a reliable A 49 and an uncomplicated route into Cheshire. 'Choosy' Cheshire, if the evidence of all the pub signs NO COACHES, CHICKEN IN THE BASKET, PARTIES BY APPOINTMENT ONLY, and the absence of any single bed-and-breakfast sign for the next thirty miles was significant—but beloved by Lewis Carroll: hence his cat. There was no shortage, though, of riding schools, race-course facilities, private fishing rights and canal cruise caravanserai. The so-called Cheshire Plain is less of a plain than an undulating plateau, on which a rolling, smooth-riding road took me close by Bunbury and rock-elevated Beeston Castle, with the Peckforton Hills to westward, into select Tarporley. Its sloping street was all 'Mrs Neal's Tea Rooms', 'Ye Olde Bun Shoppe' gabled antique galleries, coach-lamp-embellished doorways, a somewhat self-conscious collection of inherited charm. Luckily I had had a cup of tea (in lieu of 'twopenny claret and lemonade') at the shanty café where railway and Shropshire Union canal cross the road, a couple of miles before. There was a never-on-Sunday air about Tarporley.

On again through rural Cheshire, whose underground salt deposits (worked at Winsford and Northwich) in popular view give to Cheshire cheese its extra taste, by the houseless, aloof road through Delamere Forest and across the river Weaver. A time-trial rider went by, all bunched calf muscle and crackling gear change, as I rounded an uphill bend. Just beyond, in a lay-by, a car escort was recovering his empty bidon (flask). Further down, at a cross-roads, stood the time-keeper and a bunch of spectators. Two or three more sportsmen were fast disappearing up the straight. There were cheery greetings to the tourist from these enthusiasts in long grey stockings, tight breeches, black jerseys and woollen caps —but no bidon for me.

Signs now to Comberbach, to Whitley Antrobus, to Budworth Mere—Cheshire is one of the few parts of England rich in lakes, or rather willow-fringed lagoons ear-marked as nature reserves—and TO THE RACES, but little else on this carefully gradiented road. Quite suddenly it began the long glide down from the heights of northern Cheshire at Stretton, first to Stockton Heath and then to the Mersey Plain. Before I had time to evaluate the change of scene I was out of the land of no-bed-and-breakfast, over the Manchester Ship Canal and negotiating a roundabout into cobbled streets with Sunday doorstep squatters and a sign to High Quay Station, Warrington.

While the going was good and the container lorries and other heavies that take Warrington's specialities of wire, soap, boxes and beer from the factories were conspicuous by their absence. I used the A49 for the last ten miles or so, in leisurely style, by Newton-le-Willows, Ashton-in-Makerfield and Goose Green to reach Wigan. The landscape here cried aloud of the ravages of mining; through the former lodge gates and drive-ways of great houses and their parks one looked across hills of spoil, slag heaps and scattered, dirty pools to pit-shaft winding gear on a coal-dark horizon. So I rode out my day of effort—without mouth-opening or quill-sucking and with scarcely any walking—about eighty miles all told; incidentally, also, out of this chapter and into the next.

CHAPTER FIVE

VIEW NORTH-WEST

It is a good plan to remove the brake for a week or two: this gives good practice in back-pedalling. Then, if your brake goes wrong, you will not feel a distressing want of confidence.

'No,' said my landlady of the night with emphasis, 'no, I wouldn't choose to live anywhere else. It's Wigan for me. There's nowhere like Wigan Lane for warmth.' The pub was certainly that, but what she meant was what Walter Greenwood, son and shrewd analyst of Lancashire, attributed to its womenfolk—'that old-fashioned thing, a heart'. On the way out I stopped to ask direction of a grey, pinched little woman in clogs carrying a quart jug. 'Just round thur, luv,' she said, 'by th' backside o' the church.' And when I said something about her obvious risk, breasting a rushing stream of traffic to cross one of the busiest roads— somewhere between Miry Lane and Chapel Lane, near the canal—her reply 'Nay, ah doan't mind 'em: t'lads hev to get on with theer job' also implied 'warmth'.

I liked Wigan. Parts of its southern end may recall industrial scenes by Gustave Doré—all blackened brick and cindery waste ground, back-to-back houses, half-stocked little shops in dismal streets, infants' schools with spiked railings and playground prospects of colossal factory chimneys—but there are also many new developments. There are attractive flats and schools and shops on Worsley Mesnes (old rectoral 'demesnes'), a fine grammar school facing Bull Hey, and modern dwellings with playing fields and clubs elsewhere.

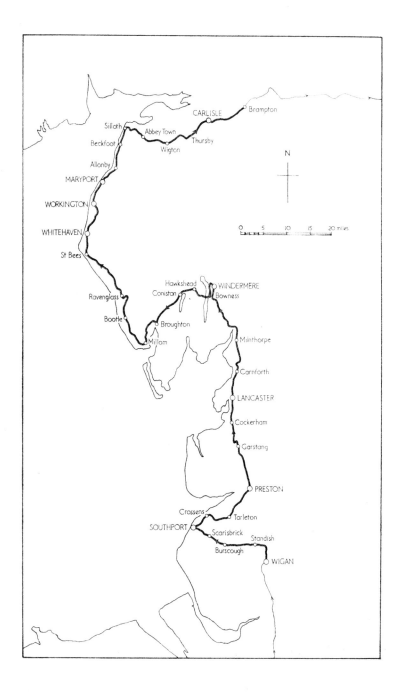

CARLISLE
Brampton
Silloth
Abbey Town
Beckfoot
Thursby
Wigton
Allonby
MARYPORT
WORKINGTON
WHITEHAVEN
St Bees
Hawkshead   WINDERMERE
Coniston   Bowness
Ravenglass
Bootle
Broughton
Millom   Milnthorpe
                Carnforth
                LANCASTER
                Cockerham
                Garstang
                PRESTON
Crossens
                Tarleton
SOUTHPORT
        Scarisbrick   Standish
            Burscough   WIGAN

N

0   5   10   15   20 miles

The centre has character—a solid, darkened stone church almost as black as if hewn from cannel* coal, with sturdy pinnacled tower, set among green lawns and rose beds; a wide and windy market place with cobbled wiends (Scottish, wynds) leading off to tight little pubs; a tunnel-like covered way of stalls—Market Arcade—giving on to the market hall and square; tall brick façades in Wallgate (one of the four medieval streets which converged at the parish church, the others being Hallgate, Millgate and Standishgate) that glow as rosily pink in sunshine as the façade of the Palace of the Winds at Jaipur. At a minute snack-bar, huddled under a road arch near the railway station, I asked for a mid-morning cup of tea and an Eccles cake—'av two, luv, while they're fresh'. This is the heart of Lancashire, a place fit for the followers of Rugby League, whose heroes on postcard photos were for sale in most of the side-street newsagents.

From the centre Wigan Lane leads out between shops and terraces—in that typically Lancashire, almost primitive building style where every stone is seen clearly and separately surrounded by white mortar and doors and windows are given similarly emphatic treatment, while the streets diminish in endless perspectives of low and uniform roofline—to more spacious suburbs and tree-lined avenues. Its character here seems not inconsistent with the town's reputation, however unlikely, as an eighteenth-century spa. (Its springs of chalybeate water became contaminated by coal workings and eventually drained away, but New Springs and Harrogate Street, near the Post Office, are reminders.) One remembers that this is an ancient borough with many layers of history, a meeting-place of Roman highways and site of a Roman fort.

At Standish, where the coal seams, which once lay rich beneath Wigan streets, are worked out, I left the A49 finally for Parbold and the coast, forking at Pepper Lane to cross the M6 near Almond Brook. After a glance from the

---

* Cannel or candle coal, found at Haigh, near Wigan, in large blocks as black as jet and capable of taking a fine polish.

bridge over the motorway at the frenzied rush below of those
for whom the road engineers reputedly include in their planning 'an appraisal of landscape quality (as viewed from a car
window) based on the frequency and duration of vision of
the particular elements in the landscape seen from the road',
I rode on thankfully to Parbold Hill. The view from the top
is extensive and in complete contrast to coalfield Lancashire.
I looked across canal, railway and the valley of the river Douglas to green flats and rich agricultural land stretching up
to Longton Marsh and the Ribble estuary. The hill drops
swiftly, almost too swiftly at 1 in 8—in the 'Tour of Britain',
1972, it was a hill climb 'prime'—to valley level in one swoop.
From Parbold village I forked left again for Newburgh,
Burscough and Scarisbeck and so into a less-known rural
Lancashire of attractive dark red-brick cottages, solid old
stone houses with porticoes, shining glasshouses, market gardens, green-verged canals and winding aim-lost roads. The
paintwork on the houses here *stayed* bright green and cream.
There were occasional wooded avenues between the immense
levels of green pasture and rich black peaty soil, landmarked
by some solitary wind-bent tree.

This is recovered land, drained with the help of Dutch
engineers, the Lancashire equivalent of Lincolnshire's Holland division. I was riding, in fact, more or less on the
perimeter of what had been once a great lake—larger than
Windermere—Martin Mere, of which Moss Side, Marshside
and Mere Brow are mnemonic echoes. It has aptly been
called 'Looking Glass Land', since in every ditch and hollow
there is the sheen of water. Pumping stations work continuously to keep Martin Mere, over which the monks of Burscough Priory formerly had fishing rights, free of floods. The
level of water rises and falls with the tide on the nearby coast.
Among the old farms and halls built on what were once
islands in the mere, one farm has a lantern turret still, to
guide the wanderer after dark. All that was missing in this
second fen district was a windmill—or perhaps it was I who
missed a sail-less stump near Burscough.

As I came into Southport by the north shore the pencil of Blackpool Tower was just visible across the estuary. First, long avenues of villas and neat semi's, then a public park and golf links, then a beach road whose surface had constantly shifting patterns of fine drifting sand. Dunes, marram-grass and a browny-yellow sea make up Southport's six miles of beach—a scene more inspiring to the water colourist than the bather: the sea, pushed back by sand, has receded so far that a miniature train on an interminable pier is needed to reach it in comfort. A large, ornamental marine lake has been built on the foreshore for boating enthusiasts by way of substitute. I coasted by the lake, 'Claud' and rider both imperceptibly coated with sand, past the amusement park, then turned left and was in the street that more than any other has given Southport its stylish, queenly reputation among northern resorts—Lord Street.

Since the first house in Southport was built in 1792 (the town acquired its name only in 1798) and the development plan was on garden-city lines, wide streets and tree-lined avenues are the rule. Lord Street is a level, gracious, chestnut-lined boulevard well over a mile long, parallel with the shore road but protected from its exposure by other blocks of buildings through which narrow 'lanes', in the Brighton sense, give access to the front. The flavour here is of Cheltenham, a Cheltenham without the retired generals. On one side gardens, arbours, fountains and broad walks among lawns, backed by public buildings: on the other a long roofed arcade, supported on slender pillars, but otherwise open with a fascinating range of shops, some with individual side arcades. The roofline above these houses of fashion and quality mingles Dutch gables and neo-Tudor timbered ones with classical pediments, sometimes with a date—1825—and period fascias with various emblems, such as a head of the young Queen Victoria in plaster relief or a pride of golden lions. Establishments like that of Waring and Gillow, world-famous makers of fine furniture, and of select antique and exclusive dress firms add their distinction. This is the parade, in season, of holiday-makers who count themselves discriminating, as opposed to the regulars of 'common' Blackpool. Out of season it is the shopping-ground of commuters, whose work lies in Liverpool or Manchester, of prosperous Jews and their wives, of those able to retire into one of the surrounding genteel suburbs. Much was done for the 'image' of Southport, between the wars, by the poster artist, Montani Fontano, whose work graced railway billboards. It is, indeed, the local Mecca for fashion, for floriculture—the annual flower show is of top rank—and for fresh vegetables. Its parsnips, pumpkins and potatoes, the latter said to have been raised here for the first time in Britain in the light sandy soil of the coastal plain, are unrivalled.

It is a place encouraging leisurely days, to promenade Lord Street, between the arcades in alternating sun and shade, to savour the spaciousness of the avenues, to explore behind the 'front' survivals from early days such as Bath Terrace, to enjoy the Botanic Gardens, the castellated mansions, or the display of Liverpool porcelain in the museum. I promised myself to come again with more time to spend...

On the way north from Southport, going beyond Crossens —where Dutch engineers built tidal gates to control the water level inland—to Tarleton, I rode between almost continuous market gardens. Roadside stalls offered eggs, flowers, plants and vegetables and glasshouses glinted everywhere. I also came across the first 'cycle path' beside the A59— scarcely used and with a surface much superior to most road edges. It sped me along towards Preston in luxurious ease.

Preston—'Priests' Town as some call it, because of its large Catholic element—drew me in to its busy centre by way of Penwortham and Fishergate Hill. There is an impressive grouping of roofs and spires as one ascends from the Ribble and a sense of intriguing old streets and squares on either side as one progresses to Town Hall and parish church. Although little of the eighteenth century remains even in Fishergate—most building activity came soon after Waterloo and new schemes have effectively obliterated old—Winckley

Square is a quiet backwater and there are Victorian streets of setts and blackened stone cottages within a stone's throw of the main shopping thoroughfare. I walked down one narrow side street, where an Oxfam shop faced a 'Love Aid' shop ('Look around: don't be afraid to ask for whatever you want') near the centre, and was soon in a Lowry townscape of cast-iron lamp-posts and corner grocers, scrubbed doorsteps and factory chimneys. It was a scene befitting the home of Arkwright, inventor of the water-powered spinning-frame, of Horrocks, the manufacturer of muslins and, later, of one of Courtaulds' biggest enterprises. (Later still this was also the home of the first jet-propelled bomber, the 'Canberra'.)

Preston was always a busy market town and still is. In former days a horse market was held in Fishergate, a cattle market in Church Street, a swine market close by the church, a leather and earthenware market in Cheapside, and sheep were sold on one side of the market square: there were ranges of stalls for cloth, hosiery, shoes, etc, 'fish all in a row upon the fish stones', butter, of course, and cheese, poultry and pots about the Butter Cross, apart from the various stalls of pedlars and the early morning linen and evening yarn markets. 'Shopping precincts' and bright new market complexes, which seem more like giant emporia with miniature shops instead of counters, have largely replaced such markets nowadays. Preston had recently opened a £1 million market, with an upper approach that resembles a cricket pavilion. As one bystander said: 'No, Dad, open markets are all done away with. Thur's new market, covered in: so stalls' rent is higher and prices is higher, see?' I did.

Preston disgorged me again via Friargate, by which people from the pig and poultry farming district of the Fylde came into town, and so on to the A6, a continuation of the A49, for a ride anything but peaceful as far as Garstang. From the company of cotton mills and engineering works and an endless maze of brick tenements, and from the ancillary activity that they generate on the roads, even though there was the consolation of Pennine fells to my right, I was glad to escape into an island of comparative quiet beside the river Wyre. Garstang has been doubly fortunate. Its main street ceased to be part of the highway from Preston to Lancaster forty years ago when the A6 by-pass was built on one side, and now the M6 whisks through-traffic past the town on the other side Not that the town is unbusy: the fact that it no longer straddles a trunk road seems to attract more people *to* it for its own sake, instead of merely *through* it. Eventually, it seems, the High Street and market-place will have to be turned into a pedestrian precinct—to overcome congestion.

I found this brisk little town, with its medley of wiends off the main street, as warm in atmosphere as Wigan. It is full of pubs and cafés and features which give a sense of community. The modest stone Town Hall, built in 1755, and the old market building that adjoins it have a domestic air: the market cross still stands in position, now just a pillar, before the Royal Oak—an inn featured in one of his stories by the Victorian novelist William Black, who stayed there. There is a clogger's shop—clogs being worn locally by farm workers—an attractive row of old cottages, once Callaghan's Lodging House for navvies. The old Grammar School, built in 1756, has been brought back into use as an Arts Centre and, in Thomas's Wiend, a former long-distance truck driver has turned art dealer. Only a discount store with the look of a converted cinema seems out of keeping. The canal basin— the Lancaster Canal reached the town in the 1790s by an aqueduct across the Wyre—has its old wharf and former tithe-barn: the Wyre banks form a pleasing background to the car park.

Here was a place to enjoy for a few more hours, a northern type of 'Borchester'. I chose my pub and settled in. 'Nothing like the bike on the old roads,' said my host, 'but today diesel fumes kill you.' I could not quite agree, but it does not do to start an argument with a Lancashire man—especially if you are Yorkshire!

✻   ✻   ✻

Page 143 On the Lancashire boundary—a Lakeland landmark

Page 144 (above) Newcastle-upon-Tyne, showing the swing bridge and the Guildhall (with white clock turret) beyond. On the right is the City end of the Tyne Bridge and the tower and spire of All Saints Church, built in 1796; *(below)* Durham from Bede College. showing the familiar skyline dominated by the noble Norman cathedral and castle

At Garstang the romantic hero of William Black's novel *The Strange Adventures of a Phaeton* walked at dusk by the Wyre 'in a wonderful pale green twilight' and again, later, by the canal 'gold-rippled in the moonlight' and found there the 'best ale he had drunk since he started'. Although it had not quite that effect on me it started me off in good spirits for other companionable places next morning, or it may have been the black pudding with my breakfast egg and bacon! First along the B5272 to Forton, stretched out with cottages, farms and orchards on a quiet road by a tranquil reach of canal. Its Independent Chapel (followed on the site by that of the Congregationalists) has a well-filled graveyard of eighteenth-century tombstones and verse memorials and a picturesque school, 1836, above the old hearse-house. Forton once had a black felt-hat factory—until the board school was built on its site, and handloom weavers of fine linen occupied the cottages.

Back then on route to Cockerham and Conder Green, whose houses, some new, some old—one farmhouse with massive, stepped chimney and mullioned windows has a seventeenth-century datestone—stand away from the river and the limit of the highest tides. A long low inn, the Stork, and sheep on the village green complete Conder Green, with the pale estuary of the Lune just beyond.

So I came to the county town, landmarked by the high-rise buildings of the new university and by the crowning dome of the Observatory, an impressive approach with an arm of the sea close by and the smoky-grey spread of buildings plainly in view for the last three miles. Lancaster's other eye-catcher is the commanding pile of John of Gaunt's castle, but in the town itself there seemed less of distinction than this promise. The old highway from Scotforth, with castle and church at the end of it, has many buildings along its length which knew stage and post-coach traffic, but its discreet, grey stone eighteenth-century houses, its Georgian inn, its courtyard of almshouses and their tiny chapel are too soon crowded out by tall modern buildings. Church Street at the

end of Castle Hill has some fine gentlemen's houses and the
Judge's Lodging at the foot of church steps, but the turn to
the right into Market Street and Market Square brought me
into a rather inglorious assembly of multiple stores, snack
bars, cheap tailors and the like—certain antidote to county-
town atmosphere. The former good Georgian Town Hall in
Market Square is now a museum—there is a new Town Hall
in Dalton Square—so that what was the centre of civic life
has yielded place to other interests, chiefly commercial. Off
Market Square I found a few old alleys and inns and behind
them a covered market. 'Burr round to the right, mate, and
through that ginnel' said a Lancastrian giving me its direction.

Otherwise old Lancaster can be best envisaged in bits, in
Damside and Cable Street near the bus station, in Rosemary
Lane and Cheapside, beyond St John's church, and in St
George's Quay, by the railway bridge, where the Georgian
Customs House survives and where the mahogany for Waring
and Gillow's fine furniture once was landed, on the doorstep
of their works, along with fustic, cocoa, cotton, Jamaica rum
and Antigua sugar.

After coffee and roll in a log-cabin-styled snack-bar, where
wan, baggy-eyed Lancastrian women shoppers laced their fish
and chips with the various bottled sauces and, as I came out,
a pavement voice begged 'Mister, 'av yer a penny for a cup of
tea?', I left town centre for Skerton Bridge and the Kendal
road. Demolition had dealt with most of the early buildings
about there and in Bridge Lane—something, here as elsewhere, that would not irk as much if their modern substitutes
were as dignified, harmonious and, if not characterful, at least
aesthetically inoffensive. But the Lune had the old sea-going
ambience—gulls, tied-up boats, shining reaches of mud and a
flowing tide, and an ozone no longer tainted by wafts from the
linoleum works. There, with a backward glance at what
William Black, just a hundred years earlier, called a 'clean,
bright, picturesque town' in a country 'that lies grey under
the grey portion of the heavens', and at the 'noble castellated

palace' (Castle = County Gaol) crowning the hill, I joined the A 6 traffic north. 'Proud as Preston' they say: perhaps Lancaster needs to take a bit more pride.

There was every encouragement now to get on, out of the ceaseless flow and up into Lancashire's picturesque region. First Slyne and Bolton-le-Sands, attractive villages with grey stone houses going back to the seventeenth-century: wind-swept shores with miles of firm sand on the left, rolling hills and green wooded slopes to the right. Then Carnforth (or Carnford = ford of the cranes or herons), a place for railway enthusiasts: it has a vintage set of rolling stock, station equipment and installations permanently on show. Beyond Carnforth the countryside began to change: as gritstone gave place to limestone there came greater variety and beauty of scene.

I took a by-road here for three or four miles, to Warton, Yealand Conyers and Yealand Redmayne. Warton Crag dominated the landscape, eaten away at its southern edge by quarries, but rising terrace by terrace, step and limestone ledge to the Beacon. Warton is little more than an overgrown village, but its gently rising, curving main street with old grammar school and inn, old shops and cottage bearing their date-stones, leads to a new housing estate at 'town head' and the large freestone church on the hill is far too considerable for a village. Here in the church is Warton's claim to fame. The stars and stripes of the Washington family arms (ances-tors of George Washington), formerly on a weathered shield on the church tower, gave the pattern adopted by the United States of America for their national flag.

With a touch of midday sun to warm the stone the Yealands looked delectable places to live in. Yealand Conyers is beauti-fully situated among limestone pastures with a distant blue mountain view—of Ingleborough, 2,373 feet—and seemingly flawless houses and cottages. It has been associated for at least three hundred years with Quakers, and something of the Friends' quiet serenity attaches to it. Traversing the high level lanes here, in and out of woodlands, interspersed with vast boulders and limestone ledges covered in ferns and creepers, was well worth the little extra effort.

Beetham and Milnthorpe, although on the highway north, have both preserved considerable charm. Beetham's Queen Anne and Georgian houses stand within parkland, on the out-skirts, but the village itself is dignified by eighteenth-century houses with finely designed doorways, all in silvery-grey stone, and a well-placed decorated church tower. Milnthorpe's mar-ket square and old market cross on three steps, overlooked by old houses, is probably not greatly changed from the 'Mill-throp' from which Thomas Gray once rode out after dinner to see the iron-forge near Sizergh and hear the thumping of huge hammers. Iron then was brought to Milnthorpe from Scotland by sea—the town being chief port of Westmorland, via the Kent estuary—and there was ship-building and gunpowder trade also to account for its appearance of a former prosperity.

From here, between the tall, grey eighteenth-century houses, which soon gave place to modern ones with sloping rock gardens, I pushed the last mile or two north on 'Princes Way', wide, spacious and made for speed, beyond Heversham until at Leven's Bridge came the sharp left turn TO THE LAKES.

Levens Hall provides a garden student's paradise. Its formal paths were designed and its topiary yews first shaped—to the likeness of the courtiers of St James—by the royal gardener in the reign of James II. Behind the high boun-dary wall its espalier fruit trees have sunned themselves for centuries. The day in question did not happen to be an open one for the grounds, so I admired the long avenue of majestic beeches and passed on towards the Lyth valley.

As an approach to the Lake District the Lyth Valley, stretching up beyond Crosthwaite and Lyth along the course of the river Gilpin, has several virtues. It is sheltered, secluded, comparatively level and almost completely in con-trast with what is to follow. Looking across to Lord's Plain, Helsington Moss and the flat, reedy pastures surrounding Underbarrow Pool I could easily have imagined that my wheels were transporting me to an Irish bog. There were the same turf cuttings, peat stacks, rule-straight ways to isolated farms, arrowy water channels. Whitbarrow Scar's wooded slopes shield the western side of this 'moss': the cliffs and limestone terraces of Underbarrow Scar, like the long embattled prow of another Ben Bulben, rise 700 feet above Brigsteer and Honeybee Wood on the other.

Here in early summer are to be found bee orchids and in late summer a rich harvest of damsons, pears and apples. The whole area is a forcing house for flowers and fruit. As I rolled along the quiet lazy road, by Gilpin Bank and Dawson Fold to Durham Bridge and Damson Dene (once a YHA hostel, now a sizeable hotel), the only sound was bird cry or lamb bleat. Crosthwaite Green and Winster are hamlets favoured in situation and favourites also of 'incomers'—holiday cottagers or settlers in the district who make much of their properties. The bright gardens and paintwork, the new porches and clipped hedges show where they have alighted. Between the two places there is a rougher tumbled countryside of rocky outcrops, gorsy slopes, plantation woods and craggy knotts, minor prelude to the Lake District scene.

After twisting, dipping and climbing by picturesque 'blind' corners and solid old Westmorland farms my road suddenly debouched into the A592, which within five minutes brought me out slap against the waterside at Bowness-on-Windermere. Almost without realising, by this confidential road, I was back to home base.

From the steamer pier at Bowness one looks up the length of the lake to Bowfell, Fairfield and the Langdale Pikes—across a yacht station, the garden front of a palatial hotel, the bosky headland of Belle Isle and beached rowing boats where swans come to hand for tit-bits. It is one of the celebrated views of the district and, on rare occasions, comparison with the Italian lakes is not unjust. All, of course, depends on the weather. The visitor, however, who really wants to see the distant company of the fells, climbs to Biscay How, just behind the hotels, for a far superior view.

Apart from hotels, some as old as Queen Adelaide, some newly risen in continental style near the 'marina', Bowness is a labyrinth of small streets and shops, chiefly curio, gift, tea and antique, with little of real Lakeland character, but much of late Victorian enterprise. I called for a 'putter-on' at Tognarelli's—one of the places where hikers in boots and cyclists in capes are none the less welcome—and then took the last bit of hill towards my own 'but and ben' for the night. It is in a parish known of old for its 'statesmen',* its wrestlers, its superstitions, its inhabitants' longevity and the rather snooty inn patronised by the Lake poets.

✳   ✳   ✳

Most of those who come to the Lake District come to see and enjoy the fells and they go about on foot, not on bicycles. Before I left home base again, however, two cyclists, a young married couple from New York, stopped by. They had Peugeots and derailleur trouble, both had large sagging saddlebags, covered in plastic sheeting, and one of them carried an umbrella. Having landed at Liverpool and being bound for Edinburgh they had scheduled to 'have a look at your lakes' on the way.

One or two things puzzled them. 'Can you not ride on the M 6 then?', they asked, and 'Are there many gated roads?' Having found the former inhospitable they had tried with a postcard-sized map to steer cross-country away from it to Windermere. But what really impressed them over here was England's prosperous, non-ramshackle appearance—its farms, buildings, cars on the road, its tidiness and well-ordered amenities. 'Is everything signed so well—the footpaths, wash-rooms, 'bus stations—all over the country?' I had to admit that a National Park area took a little more care than most for tourists' convenience and that at the end of a summer weekend English tidiness might be called into question . . .

* 'Estatemen' or independent yeoman farmers.

As soon as the derailleur was adjusted and a cup of coffee drunk they were off—not into Langdale, or Easedale or Scandale to dump their bikes and see the district in the proper way, but up the straight to Keswick and Carlisle on their five-dollar-a-day schedule to Edinburgh. Like so many from overseas, they would leave with less than a coach tourist's view of the lakes . . .

Tied, perforce, to 'Claud' and a time-table, I chose another way to appreciate the unique qualities of England's playground, aiming not at the central fells but taking in almost the whole periphery, With the lake, next day, ruffled by a westerly breeze and a few yachts scudding about, I used the ferry from Bowness to the Freshwater Research Station on the Sawrey side of Lake Windermere. The two hamlets of Sawrey would pass without notice except that one contains Hill Top Farm, a small house preserved as a museum, more or less as it was lived in by Beatrix Potter. A plethora of pottery versions of her twee creatures—Mrs Tiggy-Winkle, Jemima Puddleduck, Mrs Tittlemouse, the Flopsy Bunnies and the rest—now invade every stationer's and china shop within twenty miles. Just beyond Far Sawrey, however, I rode alongside an eighteenth-century aquatint—the small, secluded Esthwaite Water, with grazing cattle, bobbing wagtails, primroses and pale lilac 'milkmaids' as the only embellishments to its pastoral calm. In the background the eye rested on the majestic outlines of Bowfell (2,960 feet), the Crinkles and Harrison Stickle, the latter from this viewpoint resembling a decapitated volcano.

Esthwaite is the lake where Wordsworth and his schoolfellows 'All shod with steel, Hissed along the polished ice'. Just beyond it, Hawkshead's square-towered church came into view, standing high above the tangle of alleyways, archways and tightly interlocked old houses. 'The Bard', a new tourist shop, had sprung up opposite the sixteenth-century grammar school, with its sundial over the door and bench carved with the poet's name—but at ten in the morning neither was open. I looked in at the unique little Methodist chapel, set inconspicuously in a corner of the square just like another house, but having 'atmosphere' and a charming gallery. Round a double corner from the square is the snug cottage—Ann Tyson's, a common local name—where Wordsworth had lodgings as a schoolboy, unchanged behind its tiny but abundant flower garden. Spinning galleries on some of the houses nearby, or their 'conversions', pointed to the days of Hawkshead's industrial importance, before machinery had superseded the use of homespun wool.

Leaving Hawkshead to its late sleep I climbed out by High Cross towards Coniston, passing another chapel masquerading as a house—Baptist this time. From the brow of the hill a superb prospect opens to Fairfield (2,863 feet): then the Coniston range opens up with the Old Man (Alt Maen—High Crag), Swirl How, Grey Friar and Weatherlam filling the whole skyline westward. I came cautiously down the heavily wooded slope, with its blind turns and hairpins, to lake level at Waterhead. The open approach and accessible shore here were in agreeable contrast to the restrictions of Windermere, where, however necessary, the signs NO ADMITTANCE, NO DOGS, NO FIRES, NO CAMPING, NO CARAVANS, NO PARKING, NO PICNICKING, begin to rankle. (Even more frequent, in season, is the sign NO VACANCIES, but tourists may well feel that only their money is really welcome.) The eastern side of Coniston Water gave promise of a completely uncommercialised lake shore. I looked down the wooded banks to Brantwood, an Italianate building owing its adaptation from 'a damp, mouldy-smelling, tumble-down cottage' to John Ruskin. He made it his home for over twenty-five years and died there in 1900. In spring the terraces and woodland walks are bright with wild daffodils.

Coniston itself has a Welsh air. Its situation, close under the Old Man, is like that of Dolgelley vis-à-vis Cader Idris: there is a Welsh-looking tabernacle tucked away behind one of the inns, old-style slatey Victorian boarding-houses, bed-and-breakfast signs everywhere, and Welsh traders among the purveyors of curios, dyed sheepskins and craftsware. With the sing-song of Welsh tourists in the two short streets, as often happens, and the presence of quarries and coppermines up behind Church Beck, the atmosphere is certainly not Lakeland Lancashire, which is Coniston's county of ownership.

I looked at the tall, grey-green slate-stone Celtic cross in Coniston churchyard, which commemorates Ruskin's life-work in a series of bas-reliefs, and into the small Ruskin museum, just behind the last shops. The series of cut and polished samples of quartz and other Lake District stones and the pencil drawings, in Ruskin's best characteristic style, of streamsides, rocky dells, gnarled trees and foliage or of a single feather seemed worth all the rest that the township today has to offer. Then, up past the road leading to the former railway station and a short stroll, from Bowmanstead, by stiled paths to the lake shore to look at Coniston's other genuine feature. This is the old Hall, once a monastery, now a farm and caravan site, whose buildings await restoration under Trust surveillance. Framed by venerable ash and oak trees it has an immense solidity—some of the walls are eleven feet thick—an ancient banqueting hall, and huge, stepped chimneys that in themselves tower taller than the main fabric. These great cylindrical grey shapes raking the sky resemble nothing so much as a battery of Dreadnought guns.

I continued along the western shores of the lake, taking many a backward glance at Coniston Old Man, looming slatily over all, and at the sturdy farms long established wherever a stream or a sheltered spot offered footing. The road ran pleasantly undulating to Torver, as the vale opened out like the Lyth valley. The fells became brackeny hills before changing to woodland—'Woodland Fell' is appropriate —while the level valley was drained by intersecting dykes. 'Lords and ladies' starred the damp meadows and before long I was looking across Mire Side and Black Moss to the Duddon estuary. Just short of it the road swung round a sloping bank and descended into Broughton-in-Furness, situated on a slight eminence above the marshes. The small square with its chestnut trees and stone obelisk in memory of John Gilpin (the donor of the site), its seventeenth-century stone houses, its couple of inns—one flourishing at the other's expense, it seemed—its church in Early English style, its welcoming cafe and expectant look—all might have come straight out of waggonette days. Broughton West (so called to distinguish it from Broughton East at the foot of Windermere) needs chestnut bloom and sun and shadow play in the square to do justice to its old-fashioned charm and its snug situation . . . I climbed out again, westwards, and took my latish break for lunch at High Cross Inn, from which there is an extensive view over Duddon sands.

The road on to Millom is dominated by Black Combe, especially in its later stages, when the feature on the southeast side near the summit that gives the name is visible from miles away. Though not a lofty mountain, nor one of much interest to climb—it is more of a bilberry picker's resort than a fell walker's—Black Combe has a commanding presence at this south-west end of the Lake District and itself commands an unrivalled view. Wordsworth claimed the reward of its turfy summit to be 'the amplest range of unobstructed prospect in Britain'. On the right day it may include the Scotch, the Irish and the Welsh coasts, Snowdon, the Isle of Man, most of the principal peaks in the Lake District and the Yorkshire fells. Those capable of identifying it may care to decide whether or not Jack Hill, in Staffordshire, is visible in addition. On this occasion my day's aim did not allow for the extra couple of hours to climb it; on another, haze coming in from the sea had made the climb rewardless.

Pedalling along, however, by ups and downs from Duddon Bridge to Hallthwaite mill, through the chaos of a road-straightening operation, then to The Green and The Hill—this last hamlet conspicuous for that particularly bright paintwork which denotes proximity to the sea—I was always conscious of Black Combe and its outlier, Black Crags, rising up almost from sea-level. It was the consolation for coming to Millom.

Millom's mining industry has gone, its iron-works closed

in 1968 and something between 150 and 200 men turn up regularly at the Labour Exchange. Apart from the main shopping centre it shows the signs—little shops shut and shuttered with rusting corrugated-iron sheets, some shops scratching on with a few handkerchiefs, sweets, oranges and apples mixed in together, left-over barbers' poles, long, bleak, brick streets with end-views of piled-up scrap iron, tips, superannuated cranes, white 'spoil' heaps. There is a Salvation Army Fortress, the RAF and Army recruiting offices and posters usual in depressed areas, an air of listless non-activity. Old women with old prams full of odds and ends stand gossiping on gusty corners: old men in tea-rooms hang on for the warmth and in hopes of being treated to a 'cuppa'. The last big event appears to have been a visit by the bishop of Penrith to open the organ—an event still advertised on every billboard.

'It's a quiet town all right,' said the young constable seeing children across the road near the railway bridge, 'but there's a grand view up t' Duddon valley from Town End.'

It was on a quiet A 595 that I headed north from Millom. The level crossing at Kirksanton, unexpectedly, was closed. I remarked to the crossing-keeper on the absence of road traffic. For once, it seems, the railways had it instead: forty or fifty trains a day, he said, came through Kirksanton with oil and plutonium (from Italy), up from Barrow to the atomic power plant at Windscale. The level run up this coast by Silecroft, Whicham and Whitbeck, on the fringe of the fells, was pleasant enough and favoured with a bit of tail wind. I looked in at the hamlet of Whicham, where the green trodden way that gives the most direct ascent of Black Combe begins. A school, with the date 1540, stood near the church and in the graveyard a stone inscribed to John Hodgson of Whirlpippin—farm name suitable for a locality so often visited by clouds and storms.

Bootle, with memory echoes of that other one on Merseyside, came as a surprise. At its lower end Old Hall, an eighteenth-century farmhouse, was painted forget-me-not

blue; the village street climbed gently uphill in a double row
of eighteenth-century cottages, past a school dated 1830; at
the further end came a pink sandstone church framed in
chestnut trees, with a sundial on a pink sandstone buttercross in the graveyard. Bootle Fell, warmed by evening sun,
provided the backcloth and from the Olde Village Shoppe
(*sic*) at the centre a lane led down between tall hedges to
another little nucleus—the Lancaster Bank (closed down),
the railway station, the post office, then on to outlying farms
and the sandy solitude of Tarn Bay. By contrast with Millom,
Bootle was idyllic.

I looked for a lodgement. The Rectory drive, just beyond
the church bore a bed-and-breakfast sign. I drew up at a
splendid brick-and-stone Georgian house, with pillared porch
and wide lawn, and pulled the bell. A young boy answered.
They had room, he thought, but the rector his father had
just got into his bath. We were overheard. From the hall,
tastefully appointed in period style, we communicated—non
sotto voce. Room and breakfast, in this genteel lodging, was
£1.30, but, to my regret, no evening meal could be provided.
Perhaps, if I looked elsewhere first: otherwise it would have
to be a bar snack supper.

I retraced the village street. There at the lower end, barely
conspicuous on its green, damp and unobtrusive board, I
found another bed-and-breakfast sign—at the Old Hall. I
sought the back door and knocked. It seemed a long time
before anyone came. Then—well, the owner was out, but they
were sure he would oblige a cyclist and they, the sub-tenants,
would be willing to provide supper—if I didn't mind sharing
theirs with them. So while awaiting the owner's return I unstrapped my bags and checked over the machine. It was
Bootle, Cumberland, TV and a roaring log fire for the night.

*   *   *

At breakfast next morning there were two hefty boys, one
hastily swallowing his cereal and toast, while his mother saw

to my sausage, bacon and eggs. It was his last school day—at Millom—before leaving at fifteen for good. His father also was off to Millom, to sign on at the Labour Exchange for the last time. He was a contract worker on building and road construction sites, and had been among the couple of hundred out of work for the last six months. 'If you finish a job in autumn there's no chance at all of contract jobs again until next spring' he told me. So, with the elder boy already added to the queue and another coming up, clear of school, uncertain of finding work, they were off, all the family, to Perth, Western Australia, the very next week, to seek a future. They had had a 'confab' with the immigration bureau at Blackpool and knew that it might be a bit rough at first—but it couldn't be rougher than to be jobless in winter in West Cumberland. Already they were busy packing, and, in fact, that was the reason for a slow answering of my knock the previous evening. So it was my turn, on leaving, to wish my hosts luck.

The breeze now blew from the south-west, cloud lay on the fells, but its lid soon lifted over the coast as I eased up the slope from Bootle to the lower reaches of Eskdale. There was a swift plunge to river level and then a climb again, angling round the park wall of Muncaster castle—where Henry VI took refuge after defeat at Hexham. Splendid deep red and pink-shaded rhododendrons also climbed the wooded slopes and 'Bird Grounds' added a feature of extra interest to a mansion, whose ownership by the Muncasters goes back to the thirteenth century, and whose great square tower offers first-rate views of the central fells. From here, in fact, in what might be called the 'underbelly' of the Lake District, one makes new acquaintance with the giants whose faces may become too familiar when viewed from Wasdale Head or Langdale. Steeple, Pillar, Gable, Lingmell, Bowfell, Scafell were half-obscured on this particular morning, as I ran down again towards Ravenglass and Gubbergill, but their bulky stance kept the eye alert and watchful for revelation.

I crossed over the private railway which runs up by Eskdale Green to Boot—a 15in-gauge line, with scaled-down signals,

platforms, bridges and all the trimmings to match, and two
chocolate-and-cream ex-SR coaches, 'Elmira' and 'Maid of
Kent', for enthusiasts at the terminus—but without seeing
'steam up'. Then over the Mite and the Irt, whose streams
are fished for salmon, and so to the lowest reaches of Wasdale.
At Gosforth, just off the main road, a notice board carried the
plea 'Will anyone interested in a local cycling group please
ring Beckermet —', a sign both of the reviving times and of
the pendulum's swing since the taken-for-granted activity of
the note in a Lake District guidebook, 1922: 'From here [ie,
Gosforth] Eskdale, Ennerdale, Wastwater and Calder Abbey
can be comfortably explored, the roads being generally excel-
lent for cycling.'

Gosforth is a bright, clean village with a bright-blue-
painted pub, shiny black-and-white shops, and two crosses in
the churchyard of Norse origin. The latter stand $14\frac{1}{4}$ feet
high and with fragmentary inscriptions to Loki and Sigun
and perhaps Baldur evoke times when both pagan and Chris-
tian faiths claimed representation. Not far beyond it I came
in sight of the massive towers and spherical installations
which represent modern scientific faith—the Windscale
atomic plant, dormant to all appearances and undisturbing
to the cows that grazed in the meadows alongside. There
were clearer views eastward now into the fells, with Steeple,
Haycock and Seatallan giving dramatic emphasis to the skyline.

Just beyond Gutterby and Beckermet I left the A595, the
direct road through Egremont to Whitehaven, for the by-road
to St Bees. A winding grassy lane, sheltered by thick hedgerows, freshened by sea breezes, led me out towards the headland. Three mares and their foals were at pasture silhouetted
against a pale blue sky, larks sang and primroses still
brightened the verges. Suddenly the lane swooped downhill
and I was at the top of a steeply pitched village street. Not
too tourist-conscious, but cared-for, not bustling, but slow-
paced and placid in the fashion of a Victorian resort, St Bees
has Georgian houses in its back lane, trim cottage rows of

weathered stone, a dairy farm with a seventeenth-century doorhead and the kind of colours in its paintwork—beech-leaf green, lilac, pale primrose—that only a seaside place can carry off. The pub in the centre that I had marked out for a snack was undergoing internal repairs—the landlord showed me another seventeenth-century date revealed on an old stair-case door—and so, instead, I went down to the beach hotel and enjoyed my shandy and sandwich in its sunny garden.

St Bees Head, its exposed sandstone face glowing red in the sun, is one of the most prominent capes on the British coast. It rises sheer from the water to a height of 300 feet and pro-jects about a mile out to sea. Large pink and red pebbles, like small, smoothly shaped round loaves, variegated the shingled foreshore. A grassy slope leads, on the landward side, up above the rocky pools and boulder-strewn base of the Head to a viewpoint celebrated for its sunsets. The name derives from St Bega, an Irish recluse, and the monastery he caused to be erected in AD 650. St Bees still has its abbey church, restored as the parish church, and a sixteenth-century gram-mar school, reconstituted in late-Victorian times as a public school. With the latter and its playing fields spreading out along the valley by the railway, and the magnificent stretch of golden sand southward of the Head, the place's prosperity seems secure. The size of the car park by the beach hotel was evidence of seasonal patronage on a considerable scale. May its village street long remain as it is, unspoiled.

There was a bluff to walk up, with the terraced plan of the village and the layout of the school gradually revealing them-selves on the sunny valley slopes and bottom, as I struck out again for Whitehaven. An airy, on-top-of-the-world stretch of road, and then I was facing Monte Carlo, or so at first glimpse its situation, its piled up roofs and sun-flashing buildings, and the sea at its elbow might have given cause for supposing. This was Whitehaven, covering with terraces and semi's the opposite cliff headland, mingling derricks and monster yellow cranes among its huddle of narrow streets down below.

A long, impressive descent brought me into the seedier

purlieus, where factory girls streamed back to work after lunch past scrap-yards and derelict sheds and the garish black-and-red Paul Jones inn. I cut away from through traffic and into narrow Roper Street. A clogger was standing on his shop doorstep for a breath of air; his window displayed clogs dyed red, blue, green and black in all sizes. Lancelot Brew told me he had once been among the eight cloggers that Whitehaven supported, all of them able to keep four men working six days a week. That was when 'trams' of coal in the pits were pushed and hauled by hand. Now that pit transport was automated and seeing that only two of the five collieries active in 1960 were still working, he had become the last of his race locally. But he was still kept too busy with orders to take a holiday, being single-handed. Clogs, always the best wear for keeping warm, dry feet in rough winters, were back in fashion again for youngsters. They looked very gay in the window with their rounded red or brown laces and shiny, nailed toe-caps.

Whitehaven, whose church contains the tomb of George Washington's grandmother, a seventeenth-century planned town, with a new quay built in 1744, owed much of its later development to the Lowther family: at prime it enjoyed tobacco trade connections with America and was the third busiest of all English ports. The port once had thriving steamer traffic to Liverpool, Belfast, the Isle of Man, just as Workington once throve on coal, iron and steel, and ship-building. Now, after long periods when over 30 per cent of the population have been workless—and almost hopeless— both towns have come to depend on a much more diversified trade and industry—the weaving of wool, rayon, and silk, carpet and furniture manufacture, plastics, chemicals, engineering components and, of course, the ramifications of nuclear fission. I did not see much of this, nor of White- haven's fishing fleet, as I left the town centre for the next climb to Parton, but its shopping streets seemed cheerful and thriving, Lowther Street being noticeably enhanced by its Georgian houses.

The road became busy and impersonal, skirting at some elevation the valleys leading seawards. At Distington I was tempted to turn off again towards the coast and so came by Harrington and Westfield, though without much profit, to Workington itself. A long, uninspiring road of drab houses formed the approach, between which, one felt, there ought to have been tramlines. 'What's the bike for, then?' someone called, as I was pushing up from the bottom of the valley dip.

Workington's picturesque element is provided by the old, narrow, brown-stone streets at the back of the town, Rosemary Lane and its links, with their junk shops, cabinet-makers, upholsterers and other craftsmen's shops. These and the dignified, blackened stone classical façade of St John's church, a smaller St Paul's, consort oddly with a modern shopping precinct, the Mace stores, large Co-ops, the three cinemas, a civic theatre, Cumbria ballroom, etc. In this busy town there seemed to be prams everywhere and exhortations to SUPPORT YOUR LOCAL SHOP, with more pubs than one could count. Those near the industrial fringe had nautical names, such as the Schooner or the Sailor's Return, and there, amid the detritus surrounding the docks, were the corner shops and stores of rough-and-ready style, that go with the demands of maritime trade. It was all rather like Commercial Road, Portsmouth.

After a cup of tea in a crowded snack bar I swung away from the new centre and on to the flat 'speedway' road to Flimby. The presence of a long wall on my nearside and continual traffic suction on the offside involved me in the general rush to get away from Workington. The faster traffic goes the faster you are inclined to go with it. In no time I was heading down the long, straight approach of brightly painted houses that does less than justice to the true flavour of Maryport. This haven under the hill, originally named Ellenport from its river, is a small, stone-built town that climbs the slope to the 'Brows'. From these (sea) brows one looks across the former iron and coal harbour—now given over to yachtsmen and fishermen; and the waters of the Solway to Criffel and the long Kirkudbright coast. There is a decaying charm about the harbour and some of the old houses alongside it which attracts the artist. I have seen pictures in oils that lent it all the glamour of a Mediterranean seaport. People used to come there from Whitehaven or Workington for a family holiday, when the harbour was packed with fishing boats, as a loiterer by the quay recalled. 'Me dad would drop his bandanna handkerchief down and they filled it up with fish, tied it and threw it up again. Then he'd drop a sixpence.'

It seemed as good a spot as any to call a halt. A grocer in Senhouse Street, who combined on the same premises second-hand book and print selling with his brisk provision trade, suggested 'about the only possible place' where, he said, everyone in town, bank managers and all, went for lunch. So I tried Harbour View Restaurant, within a stone's throw of the quay, which acted also as the modern version of 'sailor's (superior) doss'. At the weekend some of the regulars were away: so I was shown to an attic room with three single beds amid some bosomy pin-ups—to make my choice. In fact it was virtually Hobson's . . . The evening meal made up for any austerities upstairs. I was given the same as the bank managers had for their lunch—home-made soup, chicken, bread sauce, sausage, roast and purée potatoes, peas and carrots, rhubarb tart and cream, coffee.

When I came to pay in the morning, for once I questioned the bill. It was £1.25—for supper, bed and breakfast. 'People here think twice before spending their money,' explained the proprietor. 'If you want them to come again you have to give 'em value. I've been doing that over a dozen years: it pays.' No nonsense, then, about service or cover charges: and, of course, 'ambience' took second place to satisfying appetite. The cooking was the thing.

'Not much in this place for youth' had been the grocer-bookseller's comment. (He found his interests elsewhere, judging canine shows all over the North at weekends.) After an evening stroll I had to agree. If Bingo wasn't your thing nor 'The Chastity Belt' with Frankie Howerd at the local

cinema, if you couldn't claim a seat in the Sailors' Welfare
Club or a pew in the Gospel Hall, there appeared to be only
a pint at the Fo'c'sle or a pop session at the Lifeboat. Many
seemed content with or resigned to promenading the streets,
studying the news office photos, the cheap clothes, the radios
and records, the ironmongery: or larking about the uneven,
shabby side streets with their warehouse rubbish: or else
gazing from the Brows, waiting for the soft red ball of the sun
to sink behind the harbour mouth, with a final blazing track
of golden light across the estuary and its mud.

*　　　　　*　　　　　*

The run out next morning, by way of the unfinished new
promenade and across the golf links, brought me to the least
expected and perhaps the most attractive part of my 'view
north-west'. With early sun, a following breeze and the hills
across the Solway gradually clearing of mist I had to myself
an unspoiled coastline. Mild blue sea, smooth yellow-brown
sand, an edge of dune, then a wide band of daisied turf on one
side; then the coast road; and on the other side, gorse and
bramble coverts, a low ridge and beyond it pasture and cornfields rolling up to the horizon, dotted now and again with
white farm buildings. All seemed as fresh, pastoral, innocent
of developers' concerns as the morning. There were pink
clumps of thrift, blue sea-holly, large-flowered saxifrage, cur-
lews and sea-plover and a grazing group of cream, brown and
white ponies on the broad turf. This natural coastline—once
haunt of the clouded yellow butterfly—extends in all for
fifteen miles, from Maryport as far as Silloth. A few parked
caravans indicated that others, too, appreciated its freedom,
peace and charm. Only recently it has been designated an
Area of Outstanding Natural Beauty.

Entering the first village along the coast, Allonby, was
like re-entering the forgotten world of childhood. A stream,
starred with watercrowfoot, ran between the road and the
green sward, and was crossed by plank bridges to the cottages.

Where the corn mill had stood there was a dam, filled in now and grassed over. A few children's swings and a pony training track occupied part of the common, with ALLONBY RIDING SCHOOL staring large from a whitewashed gable end. The Grapes and the Ship and a large early Victorian residence with long ironwork verandah occupied most of the other two sides. A row of neat cottages, painted egg-shell blue, green and white, lilac or black and white, with seats set out in front and one in the middle acting as post office, led towards the square. It lay behind the house-with-the-verandah, was tiny, cobbled and had two houses of importance facing each other across its width. One had four grandiose Doric columns to its entrance: the other, 'Rosenhof', had been built with a portico to match, but unaccountably had not progressed beyond a first storey. From the square, side lanes led out into the country: a donkey was wandering down one of them. It needed only Betsy Trotwood... As concessions to visitors there were a hotel-cum-restaurant facing the sea, a confectioners-cum-café, 'Cottage Curios'-cum-undertaker and a house offering the more grotesque Victoriana.

One thing puzzled me—the rather grand house with the verandah, which turned out also to be the one with the Doric porch entrance from the square. I made inquiry. It was the former Bath House, to which sea-water was conducted by pipes and it may have been of Regency origin. The bath chamber and the room that was the boarders' library upstairs could still be seen. The village then had some repute as a resort. Dickens even came for sea-water baths and recorded finding 'dirty ducks in the stream and dismal old men loitering about'. Mystery solved: and perhaps some Copperfieldian echoes explained too.

After Allonby there was little change in the scene—across the water Mount Criffel (1,866ft), sea, somewhat rougher dunes, spiky grass and gorsy hillocks, lilac-shaded brown stone cottages, farmland and scattered dairy farms. Beckfoot and Bitterlees, two much smaller villages on the coast road, where a few rutted lanes meander down to the sea, were the only punctuations of tranquillity until I reached Silloth.

Like Whitehaven, Silloth, immediately strikes one as a planned town—on the gridiron pattern. It has the air of a watering-place that never quite got off the ground. There is a broad and spacious green backed by pines and rhododendrons to shelter it from the sea wind; three or four noticeably wide streets—though the vista down one of them is end-blocked by a gasometer; a tall-spired church in Harrowgateish surrounds; a corner site occupied by a too large hotel. Then, incongruously, a sign TO THE DOCKS. The pond, the park, the bright sea air, the spaciousness are at odds with the dispirited tea-rooms, the sparsely distributed shops, the unemployed men sitting about on benches. It all has an unfinished look. Why did Silloth not develop to, say, Saltburn standard and fill out this resort-type of street plan? Was it because there was no Middlesbrough and swarming population of Teesside near, or because of recurrent depression in West Cumberland or because fashions for holidays changed once the car began to oust the railway?

I had a coffee and roll in a tea-shop, where Durham accents seemed to prevail behind the counter. Noticing my bicycle at the kerb outside, a man in a choker at the next table began to tell me of his cycling days. It was during the widespread unemployment of the thirties when like many in Workington he had time on his hands. Sometimes, he said, he used to walk from there to Maryport, for a change, not for a chance of a job—the town had two-thirds of its men laid off at one period. At other times he would cycle up to Silloth. There were no cars then on the coast road: no one about there could afford even a cheap Morris Cowley. Cyclists had the whole road to themselves and with following wind used to get up speeds of 40mph and more. Great sport. Then he would have tea—'a proper tea, mind you'—at a café opposite the station for sixpence.

As I came out I noticed some kind of display in a stationer's window just across the road. It was a large folding screen completely covered with picture postcards of pre-1914 vintage—crowned and plumed heads of royalty, fluffy feather-boa'd actresses, little girls with ringlets and bare shoulders swathed in muslin, comic cards of policemen and curates, mothers-in-law and bathers. Surrounding the screen there were views of Silloth done in sepia, with strollers by the band-stand on the green, children sailing boats in the pond and all the dressy display of Edwardian holiday-makers. Those, I thought, were its best days as a resort.

The road curled inland from Silloth to circumvent the spreading arms of Morecambe Bay, where the predominant sound is the abrasive whistle of the coral-legged oyster-catcher and where gannets and waders abound. I continued the inland curve beyond Abbey Town, with its twelfth-century Cistercian remains, and on among the brightly painted farms towards Wigton. A slight descent to a road junction, somewhere near Blencogo, needed a touch of brake. There was hardly a response. I applied front as well firmly and we stopped. 'Claud', I found, had cast one of the rear blocks. A quick look back up the hill failed to locate it. So I proceeded with caution on the now busier road. The front brake would hold me, panniers and all, but not at any pace for sudden halts in traffic.*

Being without spares—a weight-saver, but rash—I sought out a back-street repairer in Wigton. Talking hard, as he fitted a substitute, about the way he used to ride from there to his home in Barrow and the unvarying pleasure it gave him—but fumbling a bit, under cover of the talk, I thought —he charged 10p and we were off. Wigton's two streets and unpretentious air, its noteworthy church by Ignatius Bonomi and its Roman Fort at Old Carlisle nearby, were not as com-pelling, this fine April noon, as the open road. Probably J. W. Robertson Scott, founding editor of *The Countryman*, who was born in Wigton, would have thought that too.

There are some outlandish names in this retiring corner of

* 'The practice of tying a branch or sapling behind the cycle to check its velocity downhill is forbidden.' (Baedeker's *Switzerland*, 1909)

Cumbria, a corner as little known to the herd as are the delights of the Cumberland coast. First Blencogo, then signs to Aglionby, Aspatria, Brisco, Salta, Pelutho, Newton Arlosh, Cargo—some, no doubt, of Viking ancestry. Farms likewise stood out in this clean, open, rolling countryside for their colourful paintwork—lime-green and cream, lilac and white, primrose and black—against the darker windbreaks of pines. At Thursby (? Thors-by) I came into the busier Cockermouth–Carlisle road and to my second sample of cycle path. It was sadly neglected and as it approached Carlisle's suburbs went up and over side-roads to housing estates and their pavement edges, with little regard for the rider's rims. A traffic sign PLEASE DON'T CLAIM YOUR RITES was the warning welcome to this northern citadel.

Carlisle's western end around the railway is seedy, with run-down tenements, junk shops, scrap dealers, cheap grocers and the like. But with the right-angled turn beyond West Walls into the city it quickly becomes capital-of-county-conscious. The centre, where old Carlisle Cross stands at the junction of English Street and Castle Street, has a Scottish atmosphere, with a rather forbidding mixture of solid banks, public buildings and serried multiple stores: there is much granite-resembling red sandstone. A Scots Free Church and not far from it Scotch Street itself are the peaceful reminders that possession of Carlisle was disputed between the English and Scots for nearly eight hundred years. After it had been granted to a Scottish king in the tenth century William Rufus claimed the city as English in 1092, Robert the Bruce attempted to take it back, and as late as 1745 it fell again to the Scots under Bonnie Prince Charlie.

The square, powerful-looking castle at the northern end, built by William Rufus, appropriately houses a regimental museum; at the southern end two conspicuous round towers, near Botchergate, rebuilt in the style of the original citadel of 1541, reinforce a total impression of dourness. The cathedral, originally the priory, which stands roughly between castle and citadel, has only a small part of the original nave to show after the ravages of siege warfare, but can boast a magnificent east window, one of the finest in Europe.

I found the narrower streets about the cavernous market hall warmer in character, and, behind the library, a fine cast-iron centrepiece of a Telford bridge, overhung by lilacs. A few interesting alleys and wynds lead off behind the fourteenth-century Guildhall and the adjacent, spick-and-span eighteenth-century Town Hall. As I was admiring them someone noticed my machine and told me about a specialist collector of bicycles in the Warwick Road. It sounded interesting. To get there 'Claud' bumped over the rounded cobbles of side streets resembling those of Preston. But in Warwick Road, a long thoroughfare starting from the Citadel, I drew a blank. At the house where I inquired, however, there was a specialist in local history, genealogy and printed ephemera involving royal occasions. *He* had once cycled from Carlisle to London in thirty-six hours and knew all about the collector of old bicycles, 'a very difficult chap to catch'.

With eye-glass on a silk cord and a 'manner', the specialist opened the introductions:

'Your name, Sir?'

'Alderson.'

'Are you a Methodist?'

'Renegade.'

'Ah, I thought as much. Lots of Aldersons up here likewise.'

'I'm an MA Cambridge,' he went on...

'Ditto,' I murmured.

'...and Damascus,' he added, 'the greater honour.'

He had once met the archbishop, it seemed, who had the gift and had given him the degree 'with a pinch of snuff'.

There was an interesting by-way here, if one could judge by the hall stairway and inner room, all piled chest-high with overflowing cartons, but I was not intending to be submerged in bygones, however esoteric.

I left Warwick Road and the brown, cobbled back streets of Carlisle for Warwick (-on-Eden) itself, a village just the other side of the M6. There was a brown-stone bridge over the river—one of the best salmon waters in England—and brown-stone lodges to the estates in this 'debatable land', which for centuries was a constant source of strife between England and Scotland. Edmond Castle stood on one side of the road, Corby Castle a little way off on the other. Fitful sun and the thunderspit of rain which suddenly blew up seemed not out of keeping in this region just south of the Roman defensive wall. I looked at my map and saw DANGER ZONE printed in red across the stretch of moorland beyond it. It was no warning of Border threat, of course, but to keep away from Spadeadam Waste and its atomic installations.

Brampton, the last little town in this remote corner of Cumberland, charmed me. Spadeadam's population influx and its position on the quieter road to Scotland—for those who prefer to avoid motorways—had obviously perked up a quiet little market town. It was spruce: a market hall painted pale and mid-blue, shops and houses nearby in light green or primrose, a pub in cherry-red and black-and-white—like some in Bruges market square—and a solid-looking house, where Prince Charles had stayed in the '45. The cobbled square is tucked away off the main road; a red sandstone church with a short-vaned spire and a red sandstone magistrate's court look across it from one end. Old street nameplates—CHURCH LANE, CHANDLERS LANE, STEPHENSON'S LANE, MOAT STREET, GELT STREET—invite one to explore. 'Gelt', I found, referred to the river, a mile or so south, and the rock there inscribed by a Roman standard-bearer.

This was my sort of town. Then why go further? A couple of big Victorian houses offered bed-and-breakfast, but they were on the traffic route. There was the Snooty Fox or the Nag's Head in the square. I chose the latter and did not regret. (The Snooty Fox, I discovered, had only two weeks before been the scene of murder.) Bed and a very substantial breakfast were £1.50—though the sheets *were* nylon, the pillows filled with foam rubber and both bath and bath-mat of shiny slippery plastic. I had dinner across the way at the White Lion, equally substantial, for £1, in the company of a French family of four on tour; then a perambulation of the cosy square again. Brampton seemed a place of good omen for starting off on my last lap and not a bad base for Common Market visitors here to view the farthest, loneliest frontier of the old Roman Empire.

CHAPTER SIX

NORTH-EAST VEIN

*If a breakdown occurs far away from the haunts of civilis-
ation, anything is better than a weary trudge, pushing the
machine, perhaps for miles.*

'YOU meet all kinds of people: you've always a word and a
bond: you see the country and you keep as young as you feel.'
This pithy summing up of the benefits I had so far experienced came from the conversation of a chance friend I made
before leaving Brampton. On the way to the Post Office in
the morning I looked in at a window display of coins, copper
ware and curios. There was nothing of great interest, but
over the half-door of the room behind the shop I thought I
saw a bicycle frame hung up. For the sake of it I went in
and soon the story came out. Here making a modest living
was an ex-member of Catford CC, a former enthusiast of road
and track who had moved, after the war, from Balham and
brought his wife to live in the place they really liked.

The frame hanging up, with its spectacular cut-away lugs
enamelled jet black on the glossy white of the tubes, was a
Stuart Purves. He had bought it twenty years earlier and had
just had it resprayed to make his debut in a newly formed
Carlisle club. Nowadays at fifty-odd he usually rode a Gillott
and was content to let the speedmen make their own running.
But in his day, A. J. Syred, this Cumbria-adopting ex-Lon-
doner, had added his name to the lists. A certificate for a
twenty-four-hour time trial, in which his distance was 372
miles 771 yards, also adorned the wall of the back shop. Apart

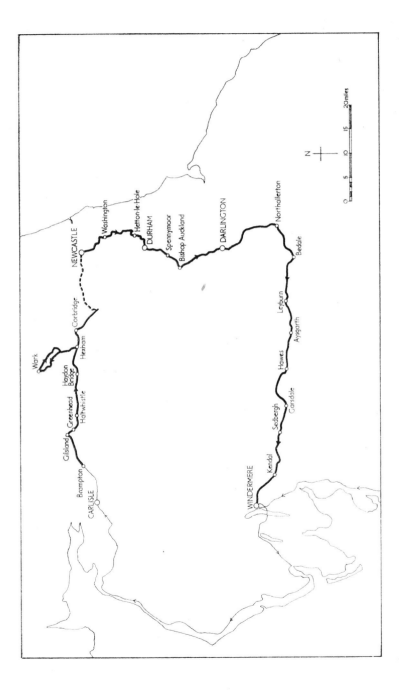

from that and a few events at Brands Hatch, he most liked
to remember the ride he had done from London to Brighton
in eight hours on a 'penny farthing'. As for giving up the
game altogether, he quoted the man of eighty who was
advised to give up cycling to work: 'Give it up?' he said,
'I might as well give up living.'

It was difficult to tear oneself away from such enthusiasm,
but after a cup of coffee in the shop, between callers—'No,
I don't buy threepenny bits, sonny, unless they're mint'...
'Yes, madam, that jug has a hairline crack'—I set off for the
'Wall'.

At the first side-turning I left the A 69 for Naworth
castle, crossed the river Irthing to red sandstone Lanercost
Abbey and then where there was a profusion of early
purple orchis on the roadside, climbed steadily to Banks.
The Wall lay just beyond—a long, exposed stretch, snaking
as pylon power cables do, straight across pasture, moorland and farm enclosures to the horizon, against a background of distant blue hills. Its wide, man-high bulk of
squared-up eight-inch blocks expressed a conqueror's confidence as well as the frontier sense of constant vigilance.
This unbroken line, eighty Roman miles long, drawn
by the order of the Emperor Hadrian across the neck of
England, from Wallsend near the mouth of the Tyne to Bowness on the Solway Firth, remains one of the most impressive
of imperial symbols. I walked on it—there is room for three
abreast—for a few hundred yards, looked across to Spadeadam Waste, White Prestor, Black Knowe and Bolt's Law,
looked eastward to Camboglanna fort (designed to hold a
thousand infantry), then westward toward Castlesteads—
and had no difficulty in deciding on which side of the wall I
would have chosen to be in the second and third centuries
BC—the *vallum* side, where the supply route ran, not the
deep ditch side where the Picts attacked.

As I continued by the road that runs between wall and
vallum (the flat-bottomed ditch on the south side, marking
the boundary of the military zone), in places the wall became

a barely noticeable grass-grown rampart with farms built athwart it and cart-ways broken through. The line was there, but, as in so many places, especially in the years after the Jacobite Rebellion of 1745, when roadmakers tore down the Roman masonry to make a foundation for *their* military road from Heddon to Greenhead, the substance had suffered. How many farms, churches, castles and cottages along the Irthing and the South Tyne have owed their building materials to depredation of this inexhaustible frontier barricade? At regular intervals on the way to Gilsland there were the watch towers, which have been excavated or whose masonry has been reassembled. It required little stretch of historical imagination to see them manned by some duty squad of auxiliaries from the garrison army—Asturians from Spain, Batavians from Holland and Belgium, Dacians, Frisians, Thuringians —whose 5,500 cavalry and 13,000 infantry etc slept, grew their corn, worshipped their tribal gods and sweated the rheumatism from their limbs in hot baths, all in the vicinity of this frontier.

Gilsland Spa—was *that* once a Roman cure centre also? In this latter day it has had more than local repute ever since Sir Walter Scott met his future bride at the village and, after their marriage in Carlisle cathedral, paid a visit to the spa and well. There was a promenade then along the waterside to a small pavilion and in due course a Spa Hotel. Out of curiosity I turned off up-hill out of the village and found a large square building in lawn surrounds, on the lip of a deep gorge facing Thirlwall Common. It was the hotel, run for a time as a miners' convalescent home, now once again a popular resort and well-booked, I learned, until autumn with holiday-makers and several weekly entertainments. Down in the village I noticed also, by Gilsland Bridge, large faded letters across the front of a brick-built house, just discernible as BATH HOUSE.

After my cheese sandwich and shandy—20p in this out-of-the-way part—at Bridge Inn I recrossed the line of the wall, near Thirlwall's mile castle, for Greenhead. Then I was running smoothly down the upper reaches of the South Tyne, by Haltwhistle, Henshaw and Bardon Mill to Haydon Bridge. Just to the north of Bardon Mill, off the A 69, lies Vindolanda (Chesterholm) on Stanegate, a road and a fort older than the wall itself, being part of the defensive system set up some forty years earlier by Agricola. Near the fort—now being re-excavated—stands a six-foot Roman milestone, thrusting up from the green turf. The leafy, lane-like road beyond Haydon Bridge—which used to be chained and barred against raiders—had another sign from the past. There was a dimly painted board to indicate steps leading down to the river bank and Haydon Spa.

As I climbed again from river level over the bank, typically wide Northumbrian views opened towards that most spectacular portion of the Wall which runs along the rim of Whin Hill Crags high above the waters of Crag Lough. A wild, rolling landscape with the mood and feeling of frontier country, where banked masses of cloud were suspended over moorland reaching back from the North Tyne to the Cheviots. It must all have seemed so remote as to be nearly meaningless to occupants of Fishbourne's Roman palace, near Chichester, basking in southern sunshine and the mild airs of the Solent—while at Vindolanda even the GOC slept on bracken.

There was an enjoyable descent by a good road past the place where North and South Tyne meet and so into Hexham. Market day was just ending: vans being loaded and stalls dismantled crammed the whole space near the Abbey; the precincts and gardens were busy with strollers; cars weaved in and out at risk. But it was nothing, said a traffic warden, to that time of the year in late July when all Newcastle's shipyard workers had holiday and all came in for the day to Hexham market. Then the pubs and cafés and eating-places were really hammered.

I asked him about accommodation and was given the advice 'Try up Shaftoe Leazes.' After one or two false starts I found Mrs Barrow of Shaftoe Crescent, who straight away called me 'hinny' and, as her husband was not working, offered easier terms if I would stay for a second night. 'Bring your bike into the hall now,' she added, 'others do.'

Hexham is friendly, bustling, no-nonsense 'Geordie' in atmosphere—Newcastle is only twenty miles off—but with at the same time something of the dignity of a cathedral town. It is spacious, solid, stone-built and much of it residential in character, particularly on the western approach. A good street of tall buildings, including Hexham House (now the Council Offices) with walled private garden and bowling green extends from the Market Place down towards the stately river. There is a colonnaded shelter in the square and a closed precinct, Fore Street and the Meal Market, both adding York-like touches of character. Antique shops have names like 'The Agricola'. On another corner of the square stands the Moot Hall, gatehouse of a twelfth-century castle. The grammar school dates from 1599. But above all there is the abbey church. Central and commanding in its green surrounds, like that of Tewkesbury, it has relics of the seventh century, an Anglo-Saxon crypt, font-bowl and frith stool. The main building belongs to the thirteenth and fourteenth centuries and contains a night stair to the monks' dormitory. The screens and the panels and misericords are notable, as are three Roman altarpieces within the church. Nowhere in the town is one unaware of this unifying and dominant presence.

The one thing Hexham seemed to lack, however, was choice of dining-out places. After a vain circuit of the likely streets I found myself in the deep oriental gloom of the Chinese 'Silver Palace' in Market Street, with a glass of Russian tea, a euphemistically named dish of pork and rice and, again, continental company. The *père de famille* asked if his bill included 'service'. Then, for a change at least of lighting, I took coffee in the one coffee bar still open at 8.0pm. It was Italian and obviously better run than most of its kind. Under the eye of the proprietor neat, smiling girls in navy blue and white dresses—among them his daughter—promptly attended to the flow of customers. His attitude,

he said, was one of service to the public. 'You must be prepared to work hard and must be dedicated to your business.'
Not only that, I thought, but you must also be seen to be—
as so few coffee bar proprietors are.

*　　　　*　　　　*

From Hexham next morning I turned north again across the
Tyne to Wall, Roman-conscious yet with its 'Centurion' shop
and 'Hadrian Inn'. At Chollerford Bridge, with its splendid
riverside pub looking upstream and its sign to Chesters (or
Cilurnum, the headquarters of an *ala* of 500 Asturian cavalry) I left the major road for one which allowed me to enjoy
the quiet villages of this secluded valley. First Humshaugh,
square-flush, stone-built with bright flower gardens, wide
verges, discreet shops and houses and an air of retirement
from the hurly-burly of such metropolitan places as Hexham. A countryside of cornfields and dairy farms and a road
sufficiently elevated above river-level to afford fine prospects
of Northumbrian grandeur saw me on to Nunwick and Wark.

Wark was the old capital of Tynedale. Its history goes back
to the eighth century and to the murder there of a king of
Northumbria. Where Wark Burn comes down from Roses
Bower and Ravensheugh to the main river there is an attractive iron lattice-work bridge and a view downstream to the
medieval tower of Chipchase Castle. The village itself is
strongly grouped about a square with chestnut trees and still
carries a sense of past importance. People seem to arrive there
as at a terminus—indeed it is, unless one wants to push on
to Bellingham *en route* for Otterburn, Carter Bar and Scotland. As I was taking my ease on a seat by the green another
touring cyclist halted there. A long, lean, weather-tanned
veteran, he had come to attend a wedding, cycle-camping all
the way from Salisbury. 'Only old hands like us on the road
nowadays.' He added, in the way that I seemed to have
heard so often, that he had given up the job he had grown
up with for over thirty years and turned landscape painter—

177

so that he could justify taking nearly permanent cycling holidays.

I should have liked to pursue the course of the North Tyne to its remotest reaches, to Deadwater in the Cheviots—just as I should have liked to follow up the Irthing river and the sign to Butterburn, Churnsike and Moscow on the previous day. But time was a stronger factor. I crossed the iron-lattice bridge and took instead the lovely, winding lanes that led downstream from Chipchase to Barrasford Castle and Cocklaw Tower, savouring again the grand expanse of this Border-stronghold country, under its great grey dirigibles of cloud. Then after a stop for a pair of Austrian car-campers, who were looking for the Wall whilst practically on it, back to Hexham and the Italian coffee bar...

The highway beside the widening reaches of the Tyne, a river that acquires European scale as it approaches Newcastle, takes one smoothly past the site of Corstopitum to the handsome bridge crossing to Corbridge. Its seven sturdy arches, built about 1674, were the only ones to withstand the great flood which swept all before it down the Tyne in 1771. Corbridge, a smartened-up little town that would fit in equally well to a Pennine background, was something of a resort in the last century. It still has that atmosphere. It lies, south-facing, on a slope above the bridge, with tall trees, a good inn and attractive stone houses, some with conservatories and rose-trellised walls that catch the sun. There is an interesting iron cross in the small market-place. After its Roman times Corbridge was the site of an Anglo-Saxon monastery and once had four churches, two peel towers and its own mint. The tower of St Andrew's church has eighth-century remains and there are Anglo-Saxon window-heads, although most of the fabric is of the thirteenth century. The vicarage here is fortified—no matter for surprise in these parts. With its three or four antique shops, its Roman associations, its clean, trim buildings and space enough to set tables with umbrellas out in front of a roadside inn, Corbridge is a place, like Brampton, to attract more travellers than those who are rushing through on the A 68 into Scotland or down towards Tynemouth.

From Corbridge I recrossed the river, by the old bridge carrying traffic only one way at a time, and after Riding Mill—where one of Northumberland's remaining blacksmith's forges is still in use—turned off the A 68 half-way up a steepish hill in the direction of Ebchester. It was a welcome change from the lorry traffic and fumes to pine-scented, sandy-verged lanes rolling gently through open farmland, with their fine outlook north over the whole spreading landscape from Tyne valley to Roman wall. One could enjoy its parallel along some reaches of the Seine. I was relishing king-of-the-road riding when suddenly, right under my saddle, something exploded. 'Claud' bumped, almost bounced to a halt. The back tyre had ballooned and beyond the rim in one place a sausage of tube was still momentarily distending. I released the valve and with a sharp whistle it collapsed. 'Flat' again. It did not take long to isolate the trouble and its cause. My talkative Wigton cycle-repairer had set a brake block very slightly beyond the serrated edge of the wheel rim, so that its friction had gradually penetrated the side wall of the tyre. Sand had perhaps finally abraded the fabric until the block edge ran on the inner tube. There was a large damaged area, worn through or half punctured, and it obviously needed a new inner. I knew that I should have carried one whatever other impediment I had scuttled. And it occurred to me how true was one, at least, of the *Rambler's* golden hints: 'With a machine just back from the workshop it is advisable to go over all parts with the spanner and tighten up any nuts that may be loose. Experience shows that workmen are apt to be very careless about properly tightening nuts . . .'

The nearest place was Whittonstall, a mere hamlet. I walked to it and stopped at the road junction. Shortly three 'Geordies' stopped also in a decrepit scrap-dealer's van. They looked as rough and tough as the stuff they carried. I caught the driver's eye and pointed to the 'flat.' He nodded and jerked a thumb to the back of the van. There was only a loose hasp through the staple. I heaved 'Claud' in and settled down on an old tyre, holding the machine upright while the van revved, then leaped and rattled on its way.

The driver's seat was open to the back, but with the engine noise, the road noise, the scrap's squeak and grind and the inflections of 'Geordie' speech we couldn't communicate at less than a shout, or any more than basic facts. They did their best. They were on their way to some Newcastle scrapyard and *en route*, but *off* mine of course, tried a roadside garage which they thought had once done cycle business (no spares): stopped in Prudhoe at a cycle shop (sales only) and finally fetched up in 'Races' Blaydon, where there *was* a dealer-repairer. I was as glad to get out there as I was grateful to them for their considerable trouble. Blaydon, though, was 'no deal' either—shop-keepers' half day and the cycle-repairer's phone at his home address didn't answer. What now? It seemed a pity to waste time in closed-up Blaydon . . . The answer was the train. I had just missed one, but the next reached Newcastle at 5.25 pm. So a few miles run down the Tyne, and instead of reaching Ebchester I was getting out at Central Station. Then across Neville Street and into Grainger Street to the first Halford shop before it closed. It *had* closed, the doors were already shut, but an assistant clearing up inside chanced to look my way. Without much persuasion 'Claud' was admitted, taken upstairs out of sight from the windows, and three young lads, all keen cyclists, were removing the chain and wheel to fit a new tube. It was a 'private' job—Halfords don't usually undertake repairs—and suitably rewarded. Before 6.0 pm I was out on Grainger Street again in the city centre road-worthy. Thanks again, lads.

Newcastle is one of the great nineteenth-century cities, like Manchester, whose faces are being changed in a huge and rapid commercial offensive on the general basis of 'the bigger the buildings the bigger returns', and vast new developments are being put in hand. In the central area much of the old city will disappear, with minimal regard for making or leaving an architectural background as good to live with for its future citizens. The central area had and still has in Grey Street (linked at the Market Street crossing with Grainger Street) a northern Regent Street—described by Gladstone as the best modern street in Britain. This formed part of an improvement plan, uniting old and new, undertaken by Richard Grainger, builder, John Dobson, architect, and John Clayton, Town Clerk, that was complete by 1839 and gave the city a fine collection of dignified and distinctive buildings. 'The finest provincial city in England' was its inhabitants' boast. The whole centre is now to be redeveloped on a scale greater even than that of the Grainger and Dobson era, to provide shopping and office accommodation, new hotels and public buildings: there will be a new inner ring road 'to cater for traffic problems undreamed of in those earlier days', as the official guide puts it, a new civic area and multi-storey car parks. The Haymarket, for example, 'will soon be transformed, St Thomas' church being dwarfed by the new Town Hall which is being built behind it'.

In the new centre the old conception of frontage development on the existing street pattern is deemed inadequate: instead there will be 'a number of precincts each designed to fulfil its particular function' and, of course, old market sites, including the Cloth Market and the old Town Hall area, will be 'recreated'. Stilt-supported and matchbox-like buildings are already in evidence, the multi-storey car-parks will soon arise. Too often already one has feared—and seen—the worst to hope for the best here . . . I took Grainger Street to the Grey Street crossing, looked again along the city's most beautiful thoroughfare, with its striking theatre portico (1837) and its great hotels, then turned down it towards Dean Street, Black Gate and Tyne Bridge. Homegoing traffic was already past its peak: I was able to snatch last glimpses of the Victorian city and the majestic shipping scenes as I crossed the tideway, before being suddenly caught up in a flurry of cars, crossing lights and buses stopping and starting. Goodbye, old Newcastle.

My road—the A1—was for Durham and the South: there

was no point in back-tracking to Ebchester: I should have continued from there to Durham anyway. After a few suburban miles and a 'fly-over' from which I looked down on the traffic artery serving the glittering high-rise, glass-and-concrete boxes of the Team estate, the A 1 gave warning signs of being about to merge with the M 1. Riding so far on this wide highway had begun to feel an almost disembodied activity, removed from all contact with actual houses and people, roadside shops or pubs. Distances and speeds were hard to assess: progress impersonal, dream-like. It was just a traffic conveyor belt, on which movement was relative, not absolute. Now 'prohibited' notices began to appear, 'interchange' notices, the complex and confusing ploy of segregating fast traffic for the motorway and 'losing' the rest. I was siphoned off up a ramp roadway to the east and the vague hinterland of Washington new town. Evening was sending long shadows ahead of my wheel.

I had the road to myself with a north-east following breeze and a sense of careering along four-lane carriageways into nowhere. Cloverleaf intersections, destination interchanges, flyovers and underpasses came and went, but I drew no nearer apparently, to any place of human habitation. The outskirts of Washington, the big 'blueprint' superimposed on the old village were still in a state of constructive chaos, with an inconclusive geometry of approach, service and through-way roads, but nothing visible in the way of identifiable township. The road tried to inveigle me, with falling gradient and smooth disappearing curves, still further eastward, but after making one U-turn across its deserted width I escaped to less insubstantial places—Shiney Row, Philadelphia, Newbottle and Houghton-le-Spring. These raw brick village-towns seemed all of a piece: long straggles of stereotyped housing on inhospitable, featureless colliery moors. The streets had names like 'Electric Crescent', 'Voltage Terrace', there was an occasional front parlour fish-and-chip shop, a plentiful scatter of workingmen's clubs, and pubs like The Kicking Cuddy, The Pit Laddie, The Brass Man and Liberality Arms.

Dusk was not far off. I tried several pubs without much conviction, and without luck. Either they were full up, had stopped doing B & B now—'not worth while', or 'the missis is away' or 'it's staff holidays' or 'we've nothin in' (to eat). My score of blanks reached eight or nine and I was still heading down the road, too far from Durham to bank on my chances there. Beds were sure to be had at Hetton-le-Hole, somebody had said. A bit off route: I tried it and found pubs again in plenty—and more time-wasting refusals. Eventually, when at one 'certainty' I offered to bed down in the lounge after closing time—the fug here was not too thick—and take bar luck for supper, if they would put me up, the goodnatured landlady rang up two more places on my behalf. It was a gesture of real Durham kindness—and, when I found my way down to one of them, the Fox and Hounds, still more kindness. The landlord was on his own, but custom was light and at 9.0 pm he set before me a substantial meal, cooked and served by his own hands. It had been a long time since my lunch sandwich at Hexham and quite a day. There can't be many tourists to the Durham coalfields.

*　　　　*　　　　*

Six young men were down betimes for breakfast next morning and all were served with alacrity before I got a look-in. They were on a two-month trainee management course with one of the local industrial giants and had to 'clock in' on the dot —with or without their eggs and bacon. Which explained why casual beds in Houghton-le-Spring and Hetton-le-Hole were so difficult to come by. Any accommodation available was snapped up by the organisers of these courses and this did provide a worth-while proposition for the publican. I was lucky to drop in for a spare 'single' as well as in finding a pub where the beer trade did not make heavy demands. My landlord's chief distraction, in fact, was the care of two splendid greyhounds, who also came in to breakfast. He had won £250 with them in the Midlands only the previous week and was taking a day off to run them in Glasgow the next day. They were obviously raring to go.

The acrid smell of colliery waste and smoke was not left behind until I reached the outskirts of Durham, this crisp and clear morning. There is a fine approach to the city from the north, between the wide green verges and stone-built cottages of St Giles, leading steeply down to the river, where the square-towered mass of castle and cathedral loom almost sheer. The Elvet bridge across the Wear just below is one of the finest medieval bridges in England. A certain grimness belongs to this group and the surrounding narrow, stone-paved streets, not inappropriate to the city of medieval prince-bishops who, from the castle, set on its rocky cliff like a military stronghold, ruled their turbulent county palatine (where the king's writ did not run) with a rod of iron.

The planners with their road construction have turned Durham cathedral into a museum-piece—just as Salisbury cathedral has been cut off from the outside world by inner relief roads—and much of the quarter leading up to the precincts, under preservation order, seems similarly out of the world. While the boating river, in a tree-bordered gorge and almost surrounding the cliff on which both cathedral and castle are built, affords living spectacle, the climb up from Prebend's Bridge takes one back centuries. I walked dreamily about the quiet cobbled lanes and narrow streets of university lodgings, about Framwellgate, Old Elvet and North Bailey, before hitching 'Claud' to the railings on Palace Green and looking in this greatest of Norman cathedrals. Its length is 470 feet, the central tower rises to 218 feet: immense strength is the impression inside as well as out. The great pillared nave and its massive columns, whose height equals their circumference, covered with grooved diaper work like those of Selby Abbey, carry grandeur almost to the point of oppression. The spaciousness and stern simplicity of the choir, the solid black choir stalls, carved in 1665 to restore the havoc caused under Cromwell, the great height of the Gothic Nine Altars Chapel, with the huge clock outside it, do nothing to diminish this feeling. By the human scale of the few visitors, Danes and Chinese conspicuous among them, the cathedral belongs to an age of giants or to one of supramundane elation and building energy.

When one comes away from castle and cathedral, the rest of Durham strikes one as hardly more than a big village, though a village with an outsize covered market, whose entrance is a sloping tunnel. As I dropped down Duncow Lane and over the bridge on the eastern side to a sedate street of book-dealers and other untrendy shops, the city seemed suddenly to have shrunk. I traversed the quiet street and in no time was at the junction for Neville's Cross and the A 1 again.

'Are you hostelling, then?' asked two boys toiling up the hill without the benefit of 'Claud's' gears. 'Where's the next one?' They were heading south for the open spaces and in this part of the north-east thought it nothing unusual that I should be doing the same, on a bike. Cars here have not yet become taken-for-granted necessities.

An uneventful glide down this now slightly forlorn highway as far as Sunderland Bridge, then I turned off for Spennymoor and Bishop Auckland. Spennymoor strung itself out dispiritedly and drably up a longish hill, with the modern type of shopping precinct midway and an air of being mainly a place on the way to somewhere else. At the top of the rise I found a miners' pub prepared to cut a sandwich and a place at the crowded bar elbow-to-elbow with an enthusiast.

He was enthusiastic about everything, cycling, talking, tall stories, 'characters' and seeing old England. He fancied a pony rather than a bicycle to ride about the country at leisure, but found himself instead just driving out to Barnard Castle, having a few beers, 'getting wind and getting fatter'. Two of the 'characters' whom he seemed most to admire had been through almost every village and town in England on foot and 'on the cheap'. One could talk and the other play the piano. Coming into a pub they bought the first half pint, started with their tales and tunes and for the rest of the evening had all the drinks they wanted free. Once as they came into a village a large carton fell from a passing lorry, which did not stop. They rescued it and found a gross of chocolate bars. So what did they do but stand at the school gates at four o'clock and hand one out to every child. Word spread about the two universal benefactors and nothing was lacking for their refreshment that night. 'Have another on me, mate: Newcastle ale, is it? It was a company hard to break out of, especially when I told a bit about my tour, but well before the rest left I was on my way over Middlestone Moor to Bishop Auckland.

Swinging round by the old castle, itself not far from the Roman Vinovium, I came into a jam-packed market square, where all Durham's thrifty housewives, china and hardware salesmen, fish and fruit hawkers, Pakistani 'cheap-liners', knick-knack vendors and nylon-stocking sellers seemed to have congregated. Shabby men offered *Old Moore's Almanac* on street corners and there was that huckster element which seems to find market towns on the eastern side of England more to its liking than those in the west. Some of the streets off the square were closed to traffic, but even they were crammed with shoppers, prams and push-carts. I could neither ride nor wheel the machine anywhere in comfort. There was a choice, between West Auckland or Shildon, for the route to Darlington: to get out of this pell-mell quickly, I chose the Shildon way.

The road now led through fringe terrain or 'non-country', not country, that is, in the shires' sense, well beyond New Shildon on the A6102. Coalyards, railway sidings, transport sheds interspersed with bits of farmland, roadworks, corner-pub parking lots and long, grimy brick terraces made the link-up between one large town and another something less than a refreshment of the spirit. 'Pleasing diversity of hill and dale, even in this d----d weather, about Darlington' wrote a traveller going north this way to Durham, by coach, about two hundred years ago—while on Morden's early maps places like Shildon and Spennymoor, before the pits were sunk, were farmhouses. That diversity was obliterated and there was only the sensed proximity of another 'Washington' at Newton Aycliffe for substitute. For the moment I sympathised with the two boys of that morning, 'heading south' guilelessly down the A 1.

Darlington was a larger, brasher Bishop Auckland. Biggish houses of seedy brick and crumbling plaster on the outskirts, a shopping thoroughfare with long perspectives of cheaper, painted-up side streets leading to the centre. Here a raised walk with seats, opposite the market, gave a small oasis of rest for laden housewives encumbered by their bairns and baskets. The market has a tall, Victorian, yellow-brick clock tower, like a Tuscan campanile incongruously crowned by a spire, and beyond it lie the railway yards and long streets, with unlikely names such as 'Model Place', corner betting shops at their entry and cooling towers as their end prospect.

I had a glass of milk in the covered market and, remembering the previous day, asked about the chance of accommodation here. 'Not much, gaffer,' was the reply, 'but you could try Sheila's place up Station Road.' So I sallied out along Station Road—and thought better of it. Since I was there I looked in at Bank Top station, whose majestic cast-iron arched roof is of better proportions than most of Darlington's more recent building. On the platform stands 'Locomotive No 1', the engine built to the specifications of George Stephenson at the works which he and his son founded in Newcastle. It has been rebuilt more than once since 1823, but still retains its original appearance apart from wheels of later pattern. 'Ah,' said an old railwayman, also admiring the intricacies of external coupling rods, valves and levers, 'if there were no buttons to press nowadays them in traction department would not know what to do with it.'

With another look at the cooling-tower prospect across a choked river course surrounded by rubble and half-finished buildings, I decided to leave the town smell and take a chance of finding an alternative to Sheila's, however intimate, in more open country.

So round the curve from the market hall and back on to the A 1 until the fork at Blackwell opened another choice—the road to Northallerton. Before long on this well-surfaced, near-level and surprisingly unbusy A 167 I was enjoying broad-acre views across to the Hambleton and Cleveland Hills. At Croft where the road crosses the Tees I stopped to look at the nucleus of a once-popular spa. The rambling Spa Hotel with its three-bay pediment and the sprinkling of Queen Anne and Georgian houses suggested its days of greater importance, while the bridge surrounds had a certain backwater charm. It was at Croft rectory that the Rev Charles Dodgson brought up his son, the future creator of *Alice in Wonderland*.

Dalton-on-Tees, Entercommon Low and High, where the road from Yarm comes in, and then at Great Smeaton a spacious green-verged village, situated on a rise half a dozen miles from the Clevelands, where I thought again of bed and breakfast. It was almost 'opening time' and so I waited ten minutes beside the likeliest-looking inn. 'Sorry, we're full up. Your best chance is in Northallerton at the Buck. Tell them I've sent you, if you like.'

I took the last seven or eight miles, between immense cornfields and fine manor estates, in almost solitary possession of this fast, even road and within half an hour was knocking at the Buck's side door. 'We haven't a bed, I'm afraid; the last one has just been taken.' Half-way down the broad market-place I found the Old Golden Lion: nobody had mentioned that. It offered at £1.25 a room, a place for 'Claud' in one of the old coach-houses at the back, a TV lounge, but no evening meal.

Northallerton is the North Riding county town and has both presence and some pretension. Its single street with the church at one end and market hall in the middle has coaching-day spaciousness and several hotels. There are a number of antique shops of the cottage type at the outskirts or in the neat row that lies further from the roadway, a newish bookshop, a circular-shaped cinema and an air of harmony and dignity about the long, unbroken frontage. People can stroll the length of the town to take the evening air without being constantly ruffled by traffic. 'It has changed for the better in the last few years' was my landlord's opinion. It looked encouraging, but what were the prospects of dining out? Well, there were the hotels or the Chinese restaurant or there was that new Indian place, down one of the side alleys. It had only been open a month . . .

I walked down through the market-place to the southern end and found Romanby Court. It was, to say the least, unexpected. A small paved courtyard, with shrubs in large pots, inscrutable silk-screened windows and two heavy, dark, polished wooden doors with elaborate brass bosses. No sign of activity. I tried one resistant door knob, then tried the other. The door immediately swung open. 'Welcome, Sir, to the Shalimar Restaurant,' said a suave young man in navy-blue double-breasted blazer, sponge-bag trousers, curled beard and white turban, bowing me into the entrance-lounge cocktail bar. The little restaurant to the right was empty, but full of memories. Here, with this young manager from Lahore had come all the trappings of Lahore's selecter eating places. Indian mats hung on the walls, there were arches and nooks like ivans between the discreetly shaded windows: candles in tall blue glass holders lit the individual tables, covered with red linen cloths and with folded red napkins set by their goblets. Oriental hanging lamps and a hidden spotlight cast shapely shadows. The young Sikh bowed again as he produced the folio-size menu in a pictorial, high-bosomed 'Shalimar' folder. 'We have all special Punjabi dishes here, Sir: what would you like?'

Murgh Tikka Lahori	(marinated chicken in Punjabi spices)
Seekh Kebab Nizami	(marinated minced lamb in oriental herbs and spices)
Batou Tandori	(quail marinated and cooked in a clay oven over flaming charcoal)

or would I prefer:

Karahi Kabab Kabuli (speciality of the Pathans—diced
                    chicken cooked with tomato and
                    capsicums)?

Then, of course, there were curries with 'Basmati rice—a
gift from the Punjab' and shish kebabs—'delicacies of Tur-
kish sultans'. It was all so very like that little place near the
Park Hotel, Lahore . . .

I settled for Punjab marinated chicken, 'dal the day' and
as an afterthought asked for chapatti.

After a few minutes' chat about his home, spiced with a
shrewd comment or two about the British in India, 'You have
taken much away, but you have left nothing,' the manager
bowed himself out. In a few minutes a handsome girl in a
brown and gold sari, which left shoulder and waist bare,
presented the chicken dish with a warm smile, brought me a
drink and asked if the chapatti was right. In the kitchen, she
said, worked a Kashmiri cook, induced to come to England
from Srinagar: he had the appropriate clay oven and flam-
ing charcoal, but he did not have many requests for chapatti.
And was the chicken good also? To be honest it was just like
other chickens I had had, from Rawalpindi to Raxaul, crisply
scorched on the outside, stringily raw in the meat. However—
where did she come from, I countered? Her parents, she
said, from Tehran, but she had been born in Bombay, then
had lived in Hendon and now was 'secretary' of the restaurant. If it succeeded they hoped to open another 'Shalimar'
in Newcastle.

Only four or five other diners came in before I had finished
my mango and guava salad and drunk a piping glass of jas-
mine tea. They seemed either out for an experience or to
impress a girl. It was a bold venture, here, to try to attract
county custom at county prices. 'We don't really want local
business' the manager had said. He had probably assessed all
too well . . . I hoped to find them again, another year, 'a truly
inimitable restaurant for oriental specialities with exotic
decor and discreet atmosphere', in a one-street northern
country town. But I very much doubt whether I shall.

At Northallerton I was within easy reach of the starting-point of my journey, York. But I felt reluctant to bring my round-England tour to an end there. Instead of winding up on a plain and perhaps anti-climactic note. I decided to recross the Pennines via Wensleydale and so reach home base.

With an early start from the Old Golden Lion—the commercials with their cars alongside 'Claud' in the coach house had set breakfast time at 7.30 am, and 'one for all' seemed the rule of the house—I was soon out of the town. It was more developed, I found, on its western side with pleasant avenues and semi's. First Anderby Steeple, then the spacious, green-disposed cluster of Morton-on-Swale, and so over the M 1 at Leeming Bar. Workmen were out gravelling the road: a long stretch had just been covered in loose chips with treacly black bitumen showing through. They were now ready to start the other half of the road and the foreman waved me on to the chips. There was no oncoming traffic in sight: I turned a blind eye—and ear—to what followed and got through unscathed down the middle.

Bedale at the opening of Wensleydale turned out to be a smaller Northallerton. A wide single-street-cum-market-place led up past the slender iron butter cross to the square-towered church on its rise. The houses and shops, rosy-tiled and of Georgian brick or stucco, with pavement overflows of goods, stood well back from the road. It was the sort of place where there is ample room to pen a few calves or pigs, or draw up farm trucks or pony traps, without incommoding anybody at all. A TRAVELLING SHOP, on its way up-dale, had taken up a pitch near the cross. To absorb a little more of this deep country town—so close to the artery of the motorway—from window vantage, I had coffee in a snack-bar, where whiffs of cattle cake competed with those of diesel oil as the prevailing indication of the customers' way of life. Most of the younger end, I noted, drank milk in this milk-producing area.

A winding road as far at Patrick Brompton and Constable Burton: open views with solid farms placed well back in their own land. Then the dale began to form, with Bellerby

Moor close in on the northern side and Coverdale coming in from Carlton Moor on the south. Horse-breeding Middleham with its 'gallops' and its unsung castle ruins faced across the elusive Ure to Leyburn and its green, terraced promenade called Leyburn Shawl. Market was in full swing here and the wide, sloping square was crammed. Not all the stall-holders were fruit and veg and nylon salesmen. The lady with the bric-á-brac, bits of china and paperbacks explained to an acquaintance that she *had* to make pin-money, while her son was roaming the USA. Among the buyers, too, there was a sprinkling of good tweeds and unseasonably brown faces, of carrying voices and cigars. I bought a ripe peach, at 4 for 12p and the quick-as-a-flash salesman put me one in a bag for 4p.

There is a stiffish bit of bank just before one reaches Leyburn, from the Bedale direction, up which I was walking, whilst on the roadside some Army apprentices, from nearby Catterick camp, split up into groups for map-reading practice.

'When I wor a lad we always *rode* down this,' came a Lancashire voice.

'Yes, so did I, but not *up*.'

The owner of the voice in a passing car with caravan in tow drew up at a lay-by a few hundred yards further on and came down the road to meet me.

'What is it—a 'Claud'? Used to ride one of his tandems myself before I got this. Before that I had a Jack Taylor and before that—you probably won't have heard of it—a Maurice Selbach tandem.'

It occurred to me then that I had not seen a tandem on the road the whole way round and to wonder why. When touring cyclists were much thicker on the ground than they are today tandems among them were not uncommon: but now that the singles have thinned out, tandems seem not merely rare but have virtually disappeared. No doubt traffic conditions, in which they are less easy to handle, and the cost of a specially built machine—which can easily be as much as a passable second-hand car—have had much to do with it. We chatted on, or rather my companion provided a non-stop flow. He was sixty-seven, he told me, and with his ruddy, outdoor complexion, strong black hair and deep, athletic chest, would have carried conviction had he said fifty. Then, suddenly, a head popped out of the caravan.

'Jim!'

'Goodbye, old man,' he said, 'lunch is ready', and sprinted off.

I had my pay-off for the short climb up to Leyburn on leaving—a lovely long glide down past the Shawl to river-level again at Wensley. Then with the moors closing further in and scars or rock outcrops becoming a defining feature of the horizon, a few easy miles took me to the long ribbon of well-cared-for stone cottages that is West Witton. The prominent step-like profile of the hill-slopes in this part of Wensleydale gives rise to many waterfalls and is a result of the varied hardness of the Yoredale series of rocks—limestone, shale, sandstone and occasionally coal—that form the valley sides above the main limestone pavement. At Aysgarth Falls this latter is exposed at river level.

My thoughts now turned to lunch too. Two pubs at West Witton offered snacks. I tried one where the landlord was retailing some humorous incident to the two or three standing at the bar. He spun out his tale and looked my way, then launched into a coda to keep his audience in play and seemed altogether too engrossed to stop. I tried the other across the road. Sandwich and shandy—the latter with a bad grace, when I declined the canned sort, 'mixing one spoils the pumps and puts lemonade in the beer'—for 22½p. But the sandwich was prime pork and salad.

The dale offered double delights: the villages through which I was passing and those on the other side of the river, Preston-under-Scar, Redmire, Castle Bolton—where Mary Queen of Scots was held—Carperby, Newbiggin, Askrigg, Hardraw, Sedbusk, that I saw, as their clusters of pearly-grey stone were lighted by fleeting moments of sun on the hill slopes. All the way from the road fork at Wensley, by

Aysgarth and Bainbridge and Hawes to the last village in the dale there is an accompanying sense of reflected scene, the near-image of what one is traversing whichever side of the dale is used; it greatly enhances the broad green prospect.

I was soon beyond Aysgarth, where cheese is the rival tourist lure to the creamy falls, was leaving the bold sentinel of Penhill Beacon behind and enjoying the perfect, quiet reach of the dale, where the road most nearly approaches the river. 'That's the way to see the country,' called a picnicking motorist. 'The best,' I agreed, relishing every mile in this pure air east of the Pennines, with memory still of the acrid, gritty after-taste of Darlington. Almost two-thirds of the visitors to Wensleydale come from the counties of Durham, Northumberland, Yorkshire, primarily from the West Riding industrial towns, from South Durham and from Teesside. The attractions are its unspoilt nature, abundance of scenic and historic features of interest, the attractive villages and the absence of organised entertainment. ('Don't commercialise the area' was the plea made by many people who replied to questions on a recent sample survey of visitors.) If one added to the attractions 'unadulterated air', it would for most of them be merely stating the obvious, a waste of breath.

Bainbridge is a village, grouped handsomely about a large oblong green with a stream running through it (the river Bain), a donkey or two grazing and the long frontage of a fifteenth-century pub, the Rose and Crown, facing south across the length of it. The Bain flows down from Semerwater, a small, sequestered lake formed by morainic dam under Addlebrough and Stake Fell. There was a Roman fort at Bainbridge, on the road that came over Ribblehead from Manchester, and there are various earthworks, cairns and enclosures.

Hawes, three or four miles further up, is by comparison a small town, capital of the upper dale. I came into it by the bridge below the church that crosses Gayle beck, juddered over the cobbles in the narrow approach way and was embraced by the tight little market-place, whose shops and

houses are squeezed together elbowing for room. Beyond it
a longish, built-up street extends to Town Head, where the
road forks for Wharfedale or the Lune valley 'ower t' tops'.
('Hause' = a pass between mountains.) From the other side
of the valley the town appears as a narrow belt of masonry,
with the church tower as its highest point. Many of the
houses along this belt have decorative seventeenth- or eighteenth-century datestones; one has the translation of a Latin
motto, preserved in black on the white-washed doorhead:
'God being with us who can be against' (*Deus nobiscum
quis contra nos*) 1668—a reminder of the visit of George Fox
to the dale in 1652 and the regular Quaker meetings that
followed, when Friends' houses had their faith blazoned on
the threshold. Other houses have outside staircases to former
'knitting galleries'.* An old smithy with a half-door caught
my eye. It was entirely covered with letters, numerals and
symbols, branded on the wood. What were they? The various identification marks of sheep ownership, with which
local flocks had been stamped and for which the door served,
incidentally, as a ready reference list.

I was loitering, with afternoon sun, in the market-place
when I noticed another unexpected door. It opened directly
into a one-room bookshop, stacked mostly with Victoriana
from floor to ceiling, over the floor and on shelves bulging
precariously into the window. There was no one in attend-
ance, but a wooden bowl stood on a little table for coins
according to the extremely low prices marked. A notice stated
that the bookshop key could be obtained at the grocer's next
door if its door happened to be locked. The shop, I found,
acted as an informal visitor's library and a gossip shop for

---

* Compared with the modern West Riding woollen and worsted areas,
the cradle of Yorkshire knitting was in an 'off-beat' area, ranging from
Richmond to Sedbergh. Here sheep-farming predominated and for
about three hundred years, while men farmed, women's and children's
employment was knitting. In 1595 Richmond alone had one thousand
knitters: during the Seven Years War, 1756–63, 'The Terrible Knitters'
of Dent, near Sedbergh, provided most of the worsted stockings for the
English Army. Special crooked knitting pins, a cowband girdle and
sheath were used and special knitting choruses memorised.

the locals: all ranged its sixpenny and shilling shelves in the hope of finding something fresh after any house sale in the dale. (I picked up an early copy of *The Voyage Out*—too late.) The philanthropic owner, a cheese factor, collected certain subject books himself and for years now had put the surplus, when he had to buy a 'lot', here at the disposal of all comers. A nice touch of dales community spirit.

Cheese production and sheep rearing are the industries of this compact community—a population slowly declining and now perhaps 800 souls. 'Swardles'—the solemn-faced Swaledale breed—are driven down the main street, though less frequently than of old, Hawes being one of the premier dispersal centres for sheep, with up to 100,000 ewes and lambs passing through the sawdust ring each year. On market day, as I could well imagine, the centre almost vanishes under a sea of cars and trucks: the whole town takes on a carnival atmosphere with stalls both outside and under cover, on the dance floor of the market hall, and an influx of farming folk from miles round to keep up a brisk trade at the four inns and half-dozen eating-places. Then the old town comes into its own among its own people and the homely wash of dialect —with tourism, its rapidly growing third industry, forgotten for the time, and also the fact that cottages and old houses for sale go, as is most likely nowadays, not to young local couples but to townspeople seeking a weekend retreat.

I left Hawes, before it took too much hold—with Lovely Seat (2,213ft) beckoning me over the 'Buttertubs', the pass into Swaledale, and Widdale Fell (2,203ft) pointing the old turnpike road to Ingleton. I kept instead to the main dale route for the valley-head crossing to Sedbergh, in the company of peaty streams and crinkled dry stone walls, with the tang—or is it reek?—of sheep farms and the nasal call of green plover and the waving of cotton grass. I had easy going to Appersett, then a gradually increasing pull as the sweeping contours of the dale closed in—up to the Moorcock Inn and Garsdale Head. The Moorcock stands as isolated as any pub

I had met with on my journey, with that shuttered and retiring look needed to withstand snow blizzards at over 1,000ft. It serves travellers who come in from Appleby and Kirkby Stephen across Mallerstang Common as well as those who are linking a tour of the Lake District with one of the Yorkshire dales.

Chiang Yee, whose 'silent observations' of the English countryside refreshed many during the war years, came to Mallerstang Edge, where the Yorkshire moors seem to end. He sat facing the gap which lured the eyes into the far distance, with blue mountains at the extremity of the view, piled up range beyond range. 'I felt I was sitting in front of an old Chinese landscape painting with all the mountains brought nearer one another to fit into the picture.' The mountains were those of Lakeland and from there, in Yorkshire, he could see them better than from close at hand in the Lake District itself, where 'there was always an impression of overcrowding and one could scarcely see the whole of any mountain'.

After I had swung down Garsdale, with the railway high above on its fellside viaducts, past Grouse Hall, Thrush Gill, Dandra Garth and all the scattered farmsteads and 'statesmen's houses to Sedbergh, then traversed that close-knit town's narrow street and climbed again. I knew the same sensation. From the bank top beyond the Lune and above Lily Mere, one looks across a great distance to the Langdale Pikes. They are oriental in shape, delicately outlined, dimly blue and, somehow, are brought near as in a Chinese painting. When I saw them I knew also that Kendal lay in the next valley from where I stood and that there my journey was virtually over. Then I found how true was the saying, for cyclists however seasoned, 'it is better to travel hopefully than to arrive'.

*   *   *

All in all, I had covered about 1,350 miles. Almost the whole way I had enjoyed fine weather, though with periods of plaguey wind and with a ration of sun rather ungenerous even for an English spring. I had had no mechanical trouble, only one unavoidable puncture, no road incidents or damage of any kind. I had set off in normal good fettle and returned in far better. I had renewed acquaintance with many places half-remembered from times before and had seen something of many others that would send me to them again. There had been as much to charm, dismay, excite, and tantalise as on any foreign tour. If I were asked, in general, to suggest the areas of England most likely to offer cycling enjoyment today, I would say 'Go east, then north'. Here are the wider landscapes, the quieter roads, the untrumpeted attractions of village, valley and sea-shore, the less formal hospitality in pub and cottage. For myself I would seek out the opportunities missed in East Anglia: but that is not to say that other parts, the hunting shires, for instance, have no unexplored delights. In England fantasy lies round the corner of almost every road, however seeming dull. And for season I would suggest the spring of the year, the time of transitions and surprises, of stored energy and green promise. For the question of company—that, of course, depends on individual personality: but going solitary gives one more relish for chance meetings and chats on the way, gives more scope for whim, one's own pace and unfettered choice. Before long the bicycle becomes a companion, with its moods and murmurings, its rhythmic response and subtle road note.

For this latter, a new machine generously provided for the occasion, and for the sense of purpose with which to use it, I would here express the thanks to my publishers which it will be clear from the foregoing narrative I most certainly owe. I shall not easily give up cycling again.

HINTS FOR VISITORS AND OTHERS

Visitors from overseas who arrive in England without a bicycle, but are attracted by the idea of seeing more of it with one, perhaps need a word or two here.

There are no formalities—licences, registrations, restrictions—in acquiring a bicycle and setting out with it on the road. It is as well, of course, to have ridden one before: it is advisable to be familiar with the main points of the Highway Code, and it is a matter of self-interest to see that the brakes are in good working order. To ride without lights and rear reflector in the hours of darkness is to invite an accident and is also an offence.

Bicycles are excluded from motorways and a few other roads where special notices occur. Otherwise the rider is free to go on his machine wherever other traffic goes and on bridleways (subject to any local byelaws), but not on pedestrian footpaths either beside the roads or in parks and other public places. Special cycle paths are provided alongside some main roads and are so signed.

For enjoyment and comfort in touring a good deal depends on having the right type of machine, with the right capabilities and the right adjustments to the rider's build. For an approach to perfection, as with a suit, it is better to seek out a specialist craftsman and have a bicycle built up, with frame, angles and components selected to meet one's purpose and physique, than to buy one 'off the rack'. The whereabouts of such specialists, both in London and provincial towns, can usually be found from their advertisements in *Cycling*, a weekly magazine, or *Coureur*, a monthly.

This, of course, requires time. But, as with suits, normal

requirements can generally be met on the spot from the club sports stock of a good dealer, who will advise and make any necessary adjustments. If he is or has been a keen cyclist himself, so much the better. One should allow not less than £50 for a reliable machine with accessories.

In some places, particularly tourist centres, bicycles can also be hired by the day: a list is provided by the CTC (see below). These bicycles are usually of the sturdy type, but should be checked for roadworthiness. A single-speed roadster might cost 50p per day, a three-speed tourer 75p, with deposit of £2 or £4 if one or other of these machines were to be hired for a week or more.

A lock, preferably a small combination, is a worth-while aid to security of the essential machine and to ease of mind on one's travels. It is also one of the 'reasonable precautions' against loss required for a successful insurance claim. It is as well to note down or memorise the combination at the start: too late when the tag has been mislaid.

For clothing much depends on season, age and taste or even fashion. But all-weather cyclists need a light, showerproof zip-fastened cycling jacket. A poplin one, direct from the manufacturer, costs about £6: a better quality gaberdine about £7. Attached hoods to match can be had for 75p, detachable ones for £1.

'Plusses'—hardwearing, near-showerproof, lightweight knee-breeches are good early spring wear: most cyclists take to shorts for summer. In either case nylon or mixture stockings (or socks) and black, *not* brown shoes. The special cycling sports shoes are not essential. A jersey or sweater, of suitable weight for the season, shirt, change of underwear, these make up the essentials (plus toilet and repair gear). Lightweight cape and sou'wester are an extra safeguard. The less total weight to carry, the better.

To take a tent, as a rule, implies taking much else besides. There are good lightweight tents (under 4lb weight) complete with poles and pegs, for under £20 and these are quite roomy. But camping needs add another element and, in practice, alter both touring tempo and scope ...

There are many advantages, for new entrant and old hand alike, in becoming a member of the CTC (Cyclists' Touring Club). Membership at present costs £2 plus VAT for adults, less for youngsters. The Headquarters address is Cotterell House, 69 Meadrow, Godalming, Surrey; telephone Godalming (04 868) 7217.

Inquiries on cycles and equipment, on routes and touring are dealt with from here by HQ staff and a list of names and addresses of the firms in Great Britain and Ireland that hire out cycles for use by tourists can be obtained.

The CTC specialises in the requirements of the cycle tourist and will, on request with two or more weeks' notice, plan or suggest tours in many areas of Britain.

A special booklet for overseas visitors, *Cycling in the British Isles,* is issued by the CTC to members on request, and in the Handbook, free to members, there is an extensive list of repairers and of caterers (hotels, inns, cafés of modest charges) where the cyclist is sure of welcome. Bed and breakfast can be had for as little as 75p to £2.50, and even in non-listed places it is possible to keep within this limit. Breakfast is usually fairly substantial—fruit or cereal, bacon and eggs, toast, marmalade, coffee. Evening meal, allowing for wide local differences in demand, would come between 50p and £1, or of course more according to thirst.

In small, non-resort English towns, meal choice tends to be limited. As someone else has said, 'avoid places with a set menu, especially those half-timbered cafés and genteel guest-houses on the fringes of country towns', and for substantial meals try cottages, transport cafés, small pubs and big hotels instead of 'the middle of the catering spectrum'. Pot luck, in private lodgings, rather than soup, meat/fish, sweet, is only to be expected—but is often all the more satisfying.

The CTC Handbook is a mine of other information and technical advice—on such matters as choice of gears—for any cyclist.

Cycletouring, the CTC magazine, free to members every other month, contains many features and items of recreational cycling interest and travel, with photographs.

The CTC 'shop' at Godalming and at the London office, 13 Spring Street, Paddington (telephone 01-723 8407) offers a useful range of maps, guides and cycling books.

Finally, the CTC can provide short-term insurances, at small premium, to cover the cyclist against theft, damage, injury, accident expenses and possible third party claims. Under the Club's protective cover and with its association of 20,000 members the tourist gains confidence in emergency, besides getting a chance of new companionship.

If he is still anxious about having a roof over his head at the end of the day, membership of the YHA (Youth Hostels Association, Trevelyan House, St Albans, Herts) will ensure that, economically, in most British touring areas. In holiday seasons and popular places it is advisable to book well ahead.

INDEX